D1095163

MY DRAMA SCHOOL

Other titles in this series (General Editor: Dannie Abse)

MY OXFORD

MY CAMBRIDGE

MY LSE

MY MEDICAL SCHOOL

Forthcoming:

MY ART SCHOOL

MY SCOTTISH UNIVERSITY

My Drama School

FLORA ROBSON ROBERT MORLEY
LILLI PALMER DULCIE GRAY
PATRICK MACNEE YVONNE MITCHELL
MAI ZETTERLING ANN JELLICOE
PETER SALLIS LEE MONTAGUE
PAUL BAILEY HUGH WHITEMORE
ANNA CALDER-MARSHALL

Edited and introduced by
MARGARET McCALL

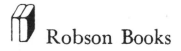

Robson Books

FIRST PUBLISHED IN GREAT BRITAIN IN 1978 BY
ROBSON BOOKS LTD., 28 POLAND STREET,
LONDON W1V 3DB. COPYRIGHT © 1978
ROBSON BOOKS.

My drama school.
  1. Drama students—Great Britain
  I. McCall, Margaret
  792'.07'1141   PN1701

ISBN 0–86051–031–X

Printed in Great Britain by R. J. Acford Ltd., Chichester.

CONTENTS

INTRODUCTION

The distinguished contributors to this book have covered between them quite a wide selection of drama schools—RADA, the Central School of Dramatic Art, the Webber-Douglas School, the London Theatre School, LAMDA and the Old Vic. And yet when they are looked at together these schools appear to be very much the same. There's the same old curriculum, the well-worn path to the stars—dancing, fencing, mime, diction, voice production, acting and make-up. All very necessary equipment for the would-be thespian.

Michel St Denis' method of teaching stands outside the norm, of course, as does the individual instruction given by Calle to Mai Zetterling in Stockholm, and by Elsa Schreiber to Lilli Palmer. But the more conventional drama school remains the backbone of dramatic training. And of this book. The variations to be found within the walls are manufactured largely by the needs and capabilities of the students, with the result that each contributor has a totally different story to tell. These were after all the most vulnerable and the most formative years of some of our brightest stars.

If RADA is represented slightly more than other schools it is possibly because it absorbed a greater number of students. When I was in America, looking towards England for a drama school, I unhesitatingly chose RADA. It was the only school I —and I suspect most Americans—had heard of. And it was Royal! As a child I'd done the usual genuflexions before the great gods of the stage. I'd delivered myself of numerous passages of Shakespeare and bits of poetry. I'd attended North-western University Speech School, and found out all about relaxation, observation and Stanislavsky. And I'd got through my RADA audition.

If RADA taught me anything it was how to get rid of my American accent. In 1949 we were encouraged to speak a totally unregional and untraceable English. Though at the time class consciousness certainly played a part in this, two of the contributors—Peter Sallis and Lee Montague—found the voice training invaluable. By erasing their cockney accents it increased the range of parts open to them, replacing the cockney not with some dreaded genteel RADA voice but, as Peter Sallis says, with 'a reasonably standard English'.

Voice production was something different, for there the bone-prop came into play. Here one learned how to throw one's voice across the footlights with accompanying sounds that were round and pure—keeping the lips and jaw well open at the same time. And that was where the miserable white plastic 'bone-prop' came in. It was placed between the front teeth where it was meant to remain for the duration of the class. I'm amused to see that Ann Jellicoe at the Central School suffered a similar discomfort. Her prop, however, 'became grubby quickly, and ultimately lost'. I had no such luck.

Most of the contributors enjoyed their training and would not have preferred any but their chosen drama school. Even Paul Bailey, who didn't have the happiest of experiences either at drama school or in his subsequent acting career, believes that it was a valuable prelude to his training ground as a novelist. And Anna Calder-Marshall writes 'there is no other training I know of which prepares one for old age', meaning, of course, that by playing character parts she gained a new understanding and insight into the feelings and susceptibilities of older people.

There seemed to be no pattern as to whether one's school was before, behind or with the current scene. From my small experience I know that schools do their best to keep up with or ahead of their times, but perhaps inevitably they are slower to change than the current often frenetic scene. Perhaps Michel St Denis was most ahead of his time. Yvonne Mitchell says he was too avant garde for the drawing-room comedies of the late 'thirties, and indeed the 'forties. 'He would,' she writes, 'have been entirely relevant to the theatre today.' On the other hand, Ann Jellicoe's Central School of 1945 was too conventional, 'harking back to 1920 or even 1910'. Even RADA sailed blithely unaware through some of the most revolutionary changes the theatre has experienced. Hugh Whitemore recognized the mid-'fifties as being the end of an era. The whole of our theatrical tradition was being turned inside out. George Devine created the Royal Court Theatre, with its epoch-making production in 1956 of *Look Back in Anger*. Joan Littlewood produced *The Quare Fellow* along with other plays, and the working class crashed the middle-class barriers, producing writers like Wesker, Pinter, Kops and Arden. At the same time the Actors' Studio was thriving in New York. And at the same time RADA stayed put, along with, I suspect, the majority of other schools.

Interestingly, though not surprisingly, the same names crop up again and again: Michel St Denis, George Devine, Glen Byam Shaw, Denys Blakelock (a gifted student in Flora Robson's day and an equally talented teacher in Montague's time), Michael MacOwan, Sir Kenneth Barnes (seemingly a fixture at RADA), Clifford Turner ... Out of these, Michel St Denis' career was—as I intimated earlier—something apart. From his experimental theatre work with the Compagnie des Quinze to Yvonne Mitchell's London Theatre Studio to the widely influential but short-lived Old Vic School, his reputation was outstanding. His extraordinary imagination insisted on a lot of animal impersonation—to test the observation of his students. Hence Yvonne Mitchell turned herself—successfully —into a penguin while Lee Montague became a chameleon (earning the comment: 'That was good, very good. But boring.').

In many drama schools there was (no doubt still is) a proportion of society girls intent only on spending Mummy's money, who regarded the place as a finishing school in which to learn to walk and talk decorously, and who had not the slightest intention of ever taking up the theatre as a profession. At my RADA, luckily, the war had changed that. When I reached it, it had been heavily invaded by mature ex-servicemen, passionately determined to make the stage their career. They had spent long hours thinking and dreaming about it; having survived the war, they did not intend to be messed about or to waste time.

Miss Brown, the secretary registrar, was used to keeping seventeen-year-old debutantes in order. She never knew what hit her. The men were 'undermining the ballet classes'. The men were 'illegally shuffling the check-in check-out cards at Rainbow Corner' (as the entrance hall was known). The men were 'removing her notices from the notice-board' (including one which had read: *For pity's sake, guard your valuables—thieves are abroad*).

Though I think, now, that my first drama school, the Northwestern University Speech School in Evanston, USA, had given me all I could absorb from a drama school, there were moments at RADA that I would not have missed. Like the one in the movement class, when Madame Sokolova asked the men to line up on one side of the room and the women on the other. One of the wittiest and most talented in the class stood in the middle, gently sagging at the knees. 'Madame Sokolova,' he drawled, 'I don't know which way to turn!' This same wit braved Clifford Turner, our voice production teacher, and delivered the piece of poetry he had chosen for that day:

> 'Now Europa was the daughter of the king of Tyre,
> And Europa was the girl who set the men on fire.
> She danced each night in the palace at ten,
> In a cabaret for Tyre's tired business men.
> *Skidilly dee . . . skidilly da.*'

It came from a current Hermione Gingold review; there were
ten more verses, each one more dubious. 'Most interesting,'
said Mr Turner. 'Next, please.'

However, the students were serious, too. I remember one of
my compemporaries objecting to a play that had been selected
for our second term. 'It's tatty, commercial, cheap, badly
written, and dull,' he said. 'I won't play in it.' (He has left the
theatre now and become a writer.) This was an unusual stand
to take, because competition for parts in a play at drama school
was as stiff as it is in the professional theatre; after all, our
future as a result might be in the balance. Visiting agents
would come to the plays, and besides, there were also the post-
production notes given by the principal of RADA, Sir Kenneth
Barnes himself.

We used to sit in a semi-circle in his office while he admin-
istered his blessing or dismissal. I had played in a rather
splendid scene from *The Beaux' Stratagem*, and had given, so I
thought, a fair display of acting and a stylish show of frills and
flounces. Finally Sir Kenneth looked up from his notes.
'Margaret McCall,' he said. 'Ummmm . . . caps awry and
petticoats trailing.' And that was all.

Such things have I inherited from my drama school. And
also dancing, movement, fencing, diction—the tools of the
trade that the contributors here delight in describing. And
though technique is not everything, it's a large part of the
battle—ninety per cent, Flora Robson would have us believe,
though Peter Sallis on the other hand boldly declares that 'no
one has ever supposed that you can be taught to act', and for
him 'technique has always been synonymous with experience'.

At Northwestern I had played Francesca da Rimini to
Charlton Heston's Paolo. At the time, I remember, I was
rather displeased that this tall, toothy Hercules who stripped
to the waist for every love scene should have replaced a more
spiritual-looking student whom I rather fancied. When the
curtain came down on the play my drama teacher was not too
pleased with me. 'Why,' she asked, 'didn't you give the same

performance as you did at the reading?' That was when I
first realized the value of technique—the technique that allows
one to play a character in the same way time after time,
regardless of how one feels or how circumstances change.

It seems clear from the experience of the contributors that
the serious student of drama needs incredible stamina, courage,
talent and grit to withstand the kind of remark made by Michel
St Denis to Yvonne Mitchell: 'Why don't you get married?'
or Peter Barkworth's to Hugh Whitemore: 'You might probably
find a niche in the theatre, but not as an actor'. The actor also
needs a keen eye, vivid imagination, hard work, dedication,
enthusiasm—and *luck*.

Just about all the contributors agree that there was one very
big gap in their so-similar training—none was given any preparation for the tough realities of theatrical life: how to cope
with the exhaustion of weekly rep, how to convince an agent,
how to sign on for the dole—in short how to survive in this
most precarious profession. At least Mai Zetterling's Calle
insisted that 'It's better to be free than secure', and 'There's
great value in change'. And these are two maxims that every
actor must adhere to or get out. Glen Byam Shaw's advice to
Lee Montague was of similar value. 'The theatre,' he said, 'is
not an insurance policy.'

For me, the best reasons for drama schools are the technical
training they offer, the opportunity the end-of-term productions
afford as a 'shop window' to agents and theatre directors (as
Peter Sallis points out, one could spend ten years in rep in the
provinces and not be seen by anyone), and the lasting friendships they initiate.

It has been some thirty years now since my Northwestern
days, yet when I invited Charlton Heston to contribute to *My
Drama School*, he replied in the graceful manner I remember so
well. 'I'm a most reluctant author,' he wrote. 'A thousand
word column looms more formidably to me than the last act
of Macbeth.' I sympathize with him. And I am impressed by
and grateful to my contributors who have selected their

most vivid memories of drama school and recorded them with
such a great deal of humour and affection.

MARGARET McCALL

Flora Robson

Dame Flora Robson was born in South Shields in 1902. She studied at the Royal Academy of Dramatic Art, winning the Bronze Medal in 1921. In 1923 she played in repertory at the Oxford Playhouse; in 1929 she joined Anmer Hall's company at the Festival Theatre, Cambridge, and says that her years in repertory in Oxford and Cambridge were her happiest times. In 1933 she joined the Old Vic-Sadler's Wells Company, playing in The Cherry Orchard, Measure for Measure, The Importance of Being Earnest, *Lady Macbeth in* Macbeth, *etc. She has appeared in a vast number of plays on the London and the New York stage, and, from 1939 on, in Hollywood films (coming second for an Oscar). In 1960 she won the Evening Standard Award for her performance in* The Aspern Papers, *in which she subsequently toured South Africa for 5 months. In the 1966 Edinburgh Festival she played Hecuba in* The Trojan Women, *and at the 1970 Festival she read speeches, poems and historical records about* Elizabeth Tudor, Queen of England. *Her films include* Catherine the Great, Fire Over England *(for which she won an award from* Film Weekly *for her performance as Queen Elizabeth I)*, 55 Days at Peking, Guns at Batasi, Those Magnificent Men in their Flying Machines, Seven Women, The Beloved, Dominique, *etc.*

She has received numerous honours, and is an Hon.D. Litt. of the Universities of London, Wales, Durham and Oxford; an Hon. Fellow of St. Ann's College, Oxford; she was given the Finnish Order of the White Lion and the White Rose for Services to Humanity. She was created CBE in 1952, and received the DBE in 1960.

For her most recent performance in the television play, The Shrimp and the Anemone, *Dame Flora was entered for the Monte Carlo Festival in February, 1978.*

From the age of five I was trained for the theatre, with lessons in elocution, singing, ballet and piano. I was one of a Scots family of seven who came to London from Northumberland. Each of us was trained for music or speech, so that we could entertain our parents on Sunday evenings.

Miss Grace Croft, the thirteenth child of a lawyer, was my elocution teacher. A girl of great charm but no money, she taught me in a kindergarten class. I had my first small success reciting 'Little Orphant Annie' at the school concert at Enfield, and she asked my father if she could take me on as a private pupil. I went to her for about a year, during which time her own teacher was paying for her first term at Beerbohm Tree's school, and I thus constituted a very small part of her income. She won a scholarship, then a Gold Medal, and became one of Tree's leading ladies, so it was natural, with her example before me, that my one ambition was to go to Tree's school myself. And so I did.

When I entered the school in 1919, it was called the Academy of Dramatic Art (later RADA). I had done no acting during the war years since I was concentrating on school examinations, and I might have gone on to Oxford but for the fact that my father's retirement and the size of our family meant there wasn't enough money. Thus, in some respects, ADA was a second choice.

I remember the thrill of excitement and fear as I walked up Gower Street for the first day of term. Dressed in home-made clothes, my hair thin and flat, I was very plain. My voice had gone slightly croaky at the fearful prospect of standing before an audience. I seemed to be surrounded by society girls, demobbed officers' wives, and rather grand older students, all of whom appeared to regard ADA as a kind of finishing school, with no intention of entering the theatre as a profession. There were a few schoolgirls like myself, and a lovely ballerina who I think later married the painter Matisse.

There were three male students and seventeen females in my class. (This was an era when to go to a dance was torture because of the scarcity of men, and you sat like a wallflower waiting to be asked to dance.) One of the men was an actor, Kynaston Reeves, who many years later played Nicholas in *The Forsyte Saga* on television. He had returned from the war and joined ADA classes in order to polish up his technique, and, incidentally, to make use of it as a shop window, for if you finished the course there was the Public Show at the Globe Theatre, to which agents and managers were invited. And if you did well there was the chance of an immediate opening in the professional theatre.

Another of the male students was a very shy, fat—and, I think, rouged—fellow, who clasped his hands modestly in front of him and never spoke to anyone. The third was an attractive he-man who could have taken his pick of any of the girl students.

We had two acting classes a week. In one we studied modern plays, which employed the whole class because the entire play was performed, with a different cast in each act (except for the men, of course, who were allowed to keep the same parts throughout the three acts). In the other class, we studied Shakespeare and Restoration plays; here the casting was more competitive, since most of the time we were only studying selected scenes.

Miss Elsie Chester took rehearsals of the modern dramas we

studied. We all admired her tremendously. At the peak of her
career she had been engaged to play the lead in a West End
production opposite Cyril Maude, when she had been involved
in an accident on a bus. Although Maude kept the play waiting
for her for nine months, her leg finally had to be amputated
and her stage career was finished. She often related the story
in floods of tears. She was temperamental and impatient with
our amateurish approach, and shouted at us dramatically, but
she gave us all a breadth of style which was useful. We came
to subtleties later on, when under-acting became the vogue.

In my first term I remember particularly studying with her
an American melodrama called *Miss Elizabeth's Prisoner*. I was
given the part of Miss Elizabeth in the first act—a dull one
which consisted mostly of exposition. But then the shy fat man
fell ill with 'flu and sadly died, just days before the play was
to be performed in an end-of-term production before the
teachers. As I was always the first to know my lines, I was asked
to take over his part as the villainous Redcoat. I learned the
lines overnight, and had a most exciting success in the production which put me into a better category and gained me a
better selection of parts in the second term.

As there were so few males at ADA the tall girls were
often asked to play men's parts, and I—with my hair tied in a
pig-tail and wearing a full-skirted, swashbuckling coat—I
looked quite passably male. It may come as a surprise that
Joan Swinburn (the tallest of us) and I and later Valerie
Taylor and that most feminine lady, Kay Hammond, were
mostly known for our male roles!

One of the many men's parts I had to play was the French
Ambassador in the court scene in Shakespeare's *King John*, in
which Kynaston Reeves played the King. Those who didn't
have actual speaking parts walked on as Lords and murmured
appropriate lines at the side—except for one girl, who had
walked on at the Old Vic (for nothing, naturally) and who
now considered herself a professional actress. As the King
died she murmured in plummy Shakespearian tones, 'The

King doth appear distraught.' We all shook with that most painful experience on the stage—suppressed laughter.

The excellent voice classes were taken by Mrs McKern. I still remember her corrections of accent, diction and voice, and I really wish that we had *fixed* accents in speech today. When a Greek chorus speaks superbly well, each member is articulating the same vowels as well as hitting the same musical note. One cannot speak *in unison* without this discipline; but the vowels of today's choruses range over such a wide scale—from the cockney 'ow' to the diphthong 'e–ooo'—that it becomes impossible.

Ballet classes (mostly exercises at the bar) were taken by that wonderful teacher, Louis d'Egville, who had taught Queen Mary dancing. There was no piano music. He just used to wander around playing his violin while we worked. I was too tall for dancing on points, and my hard ballet toes went soft in one lesson. It was agony! We were not taught to become experts in ballet; instead we learned all the dance steps. This was to come in very useful later, at the film studios, when I had to dance a gavotte or a polka or minuet. I found I could learn any dance in a few minutes.

We had elocution lessons once a week, when we were given or allowed to choose a speech from Shakespeare, and taught how to build it up to a climax. I remember my first was from *Julius Caesar*:

> 'Wherefore rejoice? What conquest brings he home?
> What tributaries follow him to Rome,
> To grace in captive bonds his chariot wheels?
> You blocks, you stones, you worse than senseless things!
> O you hard hearts, you cruel men of Rome,
> Knew you not Pompey?'

Then there were the Saturday morning fencing lessons from an expert Frenchman, Monsieur Felix Bertrand, and his aunt. We had to supply our own foils, and were instructed, of course,

in French, which I had to learn phonetically (*'tilly'*—'lunge';
'au garr'—'on guard!). Front toes forward, facing the opponent,
back foot two paces behind, turned at right angles to the front
foot, we were told; sit well down between the straddle of the
legs, place the body sideways on to the target. I never forgot
the beautiful style we were taught, though I was never any
good at it, having poor eyesight and being not at all aggressive.
However, it helped to develop a straight stance, and I am still
able to defend myself adequately with an umbrella or a ruler!

The final class, which was held once a week, was for movement only, without speech. There we were well instructed in
stage falls, and learnt to do them without injury by relaxing
completely, letting our knees give way first, and allowing our
bodies to collapse backwards or forwards. Years later, when I
was in my fifties, I had to do a fall in a film. I fell in a relaxed
heap; immediately a crowd of alarmed assistants rushed
forward to help me to my feet, and were most surprised to find
that I was not injured. Apologetically they begged for a second
'take', as they wanted my hat to fall off as I fell. I loosened my
hat and fell without injury—the hat rolling away at the right
moment. They didn't know about my early training—I could
have done a dozen such 'takes'!

We did short plays—sometimes stories that we wrote ourselves—in mime, and rehearsed them in the movement classes.
Such lessons are important, as an actor must first be conscious
of his movements before they can become automatic and
seemingly natural. How to deal, for instance, with an affected
handshake, with just a touch to the hand being proffered, out-
stretched and at chin level. Some students did not know how to
get their hands down without looking awkward. One girl, left
with her hand in mid-air, half withdrew it very daintily, and
then surveyed her nails. 'The last resort of a bad actress is to
look at her nails,' yelled the producer. For a high fascist or
Roman type of salute, we were taught to relax, bend the
elbow out sideways, and bring the hand down gently, close
to the face and body, back to its normal position. We did it

slowly at first, then faster until it became a natural movement.

Recalling my time at ADA, it is impossible not to mention some of the famous people whom we were given every opportunity to meet. Sir Kenneth Barnes became Principal during my second term, having just returned from the war. He devoted his life and talent to the Academy; he never forgot a student, and he saw every production. He always encouraged the famous to visit us; I remember most particularly Lucien Guitry, the great French player who had acted with Sarah Bernhardt and who for some years was manager of the Theatre Renaissance in Paris. His French was so beautifully articulated that even I understood a few words.

Sir Kenneth's two sisters, Violet and Irene Vanbrugh, often came and taught us deportment—how to walk well, and sit with grace and ease. And he invited many celebrated theatre people and heads of government to be members of ADA's council: George Bernard Shaw, who told him that he must always have a bishop on his council, and handsomely endowed the Academy in his will; the eminent actor, Sir Johnson Forbes-Robertson, manager of the Lyceum, for whom Shaw wrote the part of Caesar in *Caesar and Cleopatra*; the actor manager Cyril Maude; playwrights James Barrie and Arthur Pinero; lovely Gladys Cooper; Gerald du Maurier; Henry Ainley; Lady Tree; Dion Boucicault; the Honourable Charles Russell. Sir Squire Bancroft, elegant in monocle and silk hat, made an impressive President.

Throughout my course at ADA I neglected my social life terribly. This made it difficult later on when I was looking for professional work and found it hard to put myself over during interviews. However, then I hardly thought about the future. Even in the vacations I was concerned only with my work, spending all my time in our big billiard room at home, learning long speeches by heart. I soon found that Shakespeare's speeches were not long enough, so I turned to *The Trojan Women* and studied Hecuba among the ruins of Troy. This led to an exciting triumph which helped my sojourn at ADA more than anything else. It came about like this: one afternoon at the beginning of the second term, Lady Tree came to present the prizes for work during the previous term. The prize-giving was held in the unfinished theatre in Malet Street, where we had to carry in chairs for the stage and for the audience. The whole school attended. Sir Kenneth Barnes escorted Lady Tree onto the stage, and I think she distributed all the prizes within about five minutes. She then called out, 'Oh, I'm not going yet—I want to see some acting, some performances!' And she swept down from the stage, sat in the front row, and waited.

There was pandemonium! Classes had broken up, some students had left, plays were unrehearsed or totally forgotten after the holiday. Various people went on the stage thinking they knew 'To be or not to be . . .', and had to be prompted throughout. Turn after turn was shame-making. I, being a relatively new student, did not dream of pushing myself forward until Moffat Johnson, our Bensonian teacher, said, 'Robson, can't you do something?' And I burst into Hecuba's speech.

I shall never forget the generous cheers I got from students and teachers, though I suspect that they were more for the fact that I had done some face-saving than for the actual quality of my performance. The following term I won Lady Tree's Prize—five Greek plays.

Later this memory became somewhat tarnished. When I went for interviews in agents' offices that smelt of cigar smoke, I could never sell myself. Instead, I'd leap to my feet and do that 'Hecuba' speech. I'd be stopped and dispatched before I was even halfway through it.

During my second term I was given better parts, and remember playing the lead in *The Dancing Girl* by Henry Arthur Jones. It was the part of a 'fallen woman', and I had to smoke a cigarette. I had never smoked before, and even at rehearsals I had mimed it. One day Miss Chester said, 'You'd better take a cigarette today to get used to inhaling and exhaling.'

I was acting with a tall, handsome ex-Guardsman. He gave me one of his cigarettes. On the first inhalation I became very giddy, my eyes crossed, and I staggered slightly. The cigarette paper split and my mouth filled with tobacco. In my innocence I thought the cigarette was doped. However, I puffed away and flirted with the Guardsman, while Miss Chester smiled very kindly and told me, 'You'll be a very good actress, one day.'

Alas, I could never play a sophisticated role! I re-read *The Dancing Girl* recently, and could not remember a word of it, but I have a photograph of myself in the part, wearing a glamorous, sequinned dress with an elasticated hem which gives me the shape of a slim balloon. I am gazing with rapt attention at a flower.

Our classic play that term was *Romeo and Juliet*, and I played Tybalt, with three duels to fight. After Michael Hogan had whacked me over the head with his foil (I having missed the parry—luckily I was wearing a wig!), I ended up on the floor on my back, curled up in death. I was aware, as I lay there, that my jerkin had hiked up, revealing a row of safety pins that made a reef in my tights!

It was in this play that I came to know Moffat Johnson ('Johnnie'), a Scottish actor who had been a member of Sir Frank Benson's Shakespearian Company. He had been badly wounded in the war and was very lame (though later, after an operation in New York, his lameness was corrected). Of all my teachers, he had the greatest influence on me. He was so versatile that he could play the fat Falstaff and the lean Julius Caesar on alternate nights with equal brilliance. He made the characters so utterly different that his audience believed him to be two different people. Perhaps he might have become more famous had he not disguised himself so effectively. At any rate, it wasn't until he died that the critics gave him his due: his final notice paid tribute to his true stature and talent.

Johnson was very demanding and hard to please, and a strict disciplinarian—very good for us as we went through the giggling stage. As well as teaching us he would give us a 'talk-in', which made each student feel he was talking person- ally to him or her. Before we left ADA he said, 'Some of you may become stars, others supporting players. Remember, the supporters are just as important as the stars, who would not shine like a diamond without a perfect "setting". If you succeed, do not think you are a special person. You are no better than a good workman plumber. Learn humility.'

'Johnnie' was tired of seeing females in male Shakespearian roles. In protest he suddenly left the rehearsal of the play we were doing and went to see Sir Kenneth. In consequence the play was abandoned and we did selected scenes from Shakespeare instead. At last I got Ophelia in the mad scene.

However, I did have one last success in a male role, as Falkland in *The Rivals*. I have never thought of myself as a comedienne, but when I've played a comic part seriously I have often had a great success. Falkland was the first of these. (It sounds conceited to say this, but I write of myself as an unknown, in the past.) I thought the applause when I left the stage lasted for minutes, and the Guardsman, who was playing Captain Absolute, did not interrupt it. He paced up and down until it was over— nice man!

My other great teacher was Helen Haye, who won the Academy Award in 1931. She was also a Bensonian. She was slim, beautifully dressed, with that elegant walk that Royalty and some great actresses have. She could be very tart and cutting, and we had a great fear of her, but we wanted desper- ately to please her. 'Two hours of hell with Helen!' was the description of her class, yet I adored her, and it was with her that I had my first outstanding success, in Galsworthy's *The Skin Game*.

We were all hoping to get Chloe Hornblower's big scene in a boudoir. Helen Haye gave a few of us a chance to read the scene before casting, but without waiting for a rehearsal I learnt the whole scene by heart. I was given the part. I played it at several rehearsals in full spate of emotion, and was shocked when one day she stopped me and said I was boring, and started me all over again. I was to hold back the emotion, and allowed one climax only. I learned from her how to make the audience cry at a given moment. (We thought it strange that she had such great emotional power, but with her clipped voice and sophisticated manner she had never had the opportunity to display it in the theatre—until she was in her eighties, when she played the ex-Empress of Russia in *Anastasia*. This was Helen's great chance, and she was glorious.)

I came to the dress rehearsal of *The Skin Game* in a short, cheap little kimono as I was rather poor. (How many times my chances have been ruined by bad clothes!) Helen said, 'Never mind—I'll bring something else for you for the performance.' There appeared a long, elegant rest-gown made of some delicate material like chiffon. I think then I became a favourite for the Medal.

To make it all quite perfect for me, my husband in the play was Colin Clive—whose later and greatest success was Stanhope in *Journey's End*. Always a bit of a rebel, Colin thought ADA a waste of time, and went off on tour in the holidays. Thus he was already a 'pro'. He played Charlie superbly, and to my great joy presented me with my first bouquet. Weeks later he saw in my handbag a very dead pressed carnation. 'Is this one of the flowers I gave you?' he asked. 'Oh!' And we were both very embarrassed.

My other modern play success was in *Rutherford and Son*, one of the so-called Manchester plays—in the kind of part that has appeared so often in my professional life: the daughter who is left unmarried, in a world where men are scarce.

We newer students looked up to the seniors with awe and admiration. I particularly worshipped Noel Streatfeild; but, as so often happened, she didn't get a good part to show off in the Public Show, that end-of-course performance in front of a distinguished invited audience. So, unable to impress any agents with her talent, she took a job in a chorus on tour. We thought her very brave. I don't know how successful she was as an actress, but she has written wonderful books about the theatre for children, and another which, although written in the third person, is really her autobiography. I think I can recognize all the people she mentions in the book, although they have fictitious names.

Then there was Audrey Bicker-Carton, a magnificent emotional actress who used to have us all cheering and weeping. She had great elegance, and once showed us her silk stockings from Paris which had a separate compartment for each toe. She won the Bronze Medal for a superb performance in French for Madame Gachet—a marvellous teacher whose students won more medals than those of any other teacher.

Another memorable girl in my own class was called Tony Botting, very feminine, with hair parted in the middle and a fuzz of tight curls at either side. I remember learning with awe that she spoke Greek and Latin, and was a great classical scholar. (I don't remember her, however, as an actress.) It was more than forty years later, when reading Sir Compton Mackenzie's autobiography, that I learned his Greek tutor was a Professor Botting whose daughter was now the famous authoress, Antonia White.

We thought very highly of Denys Blakelock, who, when he had to give up acting owing to terrible attacks of claustrophobia, wrote for and helped innumerable young actors at RADA. Hugh Williams was another very advanced pupil, who played mostly serious parts.

We all had great 'pashes' for two of the teachers, Claude Rains and Miles Malleson, though neither in fact taught me. I still think that Rains was the greatest actor I can remember. He was, of course, very handicapped when he started his stage career. He was only five feet tall, which made him very difficult to cast. He'd get great notices, and then be out of work for ages. When he went to Hollywood his lack of height could be camouflaged, of course, though he found it hard to balance on books while playing opposite such leading ladies as the six-foot tall Kay Francis!

Miles Malleson had all the students swooning over him. He wrote a play for them, and there was great competition for the lead—and floods of tears from those who missed it. (We were all much given to tears. We thought it good for our acting.) Miles played the piano wonderfully, and all the beauties crowded round, wallowing in the sentimental tunes. Malleson is known today as the screenwriter for *Dead of Night*, *I'm All Right Jack*, *Knight Without Armour*, and so on.

I can hardly remember my last term. I think we worked too hard. I know we did *A Woman of No Importance*, for which I'm sure I was much too young to portray a 'woman with a past'. The most important occasions were the three rehearsals devoted to one scene of a play, taken by a famous actor or author. Sir Gerald du Maurier took the class through a modern play, one he was doing in London at that time called *The Prude's Fall*. I was not in the play, and watched from the side-lines. He was very much the highly polished 'French' actor, exemplifying the beginning of the style known as 'throw-away'. He was so understated, and yet conveyed so much! He was terribly unkind to the *very* English boy who attempted to play his role as the lover, and in fact openly laughed at the class's efforts. He left the last rehearsal without giving a word of criticism or saying goodbye—no wonder our hearts were in our shoes.

Another important visitor was Sir Arthur Pinero. In a silk top hat, monocle, gorgeous clothes and lavender gloves, he was a real dandy. I played yet another 'fallen woman' in a scene from one of his plays. He was kind to us.

Then came Sybil Thorndike, who directed three rehearsals of *The Trojan Women*. I played Andromache. When I burst out with a loud 'Oh God!' on hearing the tragic news of the proposed death of my baby son, Sybil stopped me. She made me whisper it. Still more terrible news was given me, and still Sybil made me hold back and stammer out a question. 'Now!' she said, 'now the audience knows what is going to happen, and you can break your heart!' I've used that technique of holding back and allowing myself only one climax again and again.

We worshipped Sybil, she was so kind and generous. When she left I cried into a towel in the dressing-room, and one girl rushed into the lavatory and kissed the seat where she had been! It was back to a man's part again for me in Shaw's *The Devil's Disciple*. I played the hero all the way through, and nearly died in the hanging scene. I remember once again having to carry chairs through to the Malet Street Theatre for the performance. It was almost completed by then, so I can say that my class was the first actually to perform there.

Then came March and the great Public Show, on which were pinned all our hopes of a Medal. 'Johnnie' gave me the part of Sister Beatrice in Maeterlinck's play of the same name. The story is about a nun who escapes into the world and is away a long time. The statue of the Virgin comes to life and takes her place in the convent. Beatrice returns raddled and tragic, finds her habit at the foot of the Virgin's statue, and dies there. I was dying of a terrible influenza epidemic. I hardly recognized my voice as my own. I think I had one good moment only, as I lay moaning over the habit.

Joan Swinstead won the Gold Medal for a marvellous performance in a French play. She spoke French like a native, and richly deserved to win. Laura Wallis Mills, the daughter of a *Punch* artist, won the Silver Medal. She always acted beautifully, and was especially good as the Nurse in *Romeo and Juliet*.

I had won several medals over my course: Lady Tree's Prize for elocution; the Arthur Talbot-Smith Prize for general excellence; the Administrator's Prize for general industry and conduct; Mrs McKern's Prize for the best student in voice production . . . and now, the Academy Bronze Medal.

We were all convinced that the Gold Medal alone meant the offer of an immediate job in a play in London. It did for Joan. And I, ill and crying bitter tears, met 'Johnnie' in a passage near the stage door. He took my arm roughly and dragged me down the passage, and when we were alone he lectured me:

'The Gold Medal means nothing! You were splendid! I'm
going to America, but if you ever need me, write! Even if I'm
at the other end of the world, I'll try to help.'

It was another ten years before my wonderful notices for
The Anatomist arrived in New York. My beloved patron wrote
at once. He hadn't forgotten his poor unfashionable student:
'I knew you would get there!' That letter was the crown of my
achievement.

One more incident to finish this strange eventful history. In
those days, actresses were elegant, well-bred and well-dressed
creatures; the famous actor-managers, too, were all gentlemen
(or if not, they soon learnt to become one), and it was perhaps
natural for them to prefer to engage Society girls. I had no
hope of work all that summer of 1921; and then Sir Kenneth
Barnes came to my aid, loyal as ever to his students, however
inelegant and scruffy. He had written a play for the ADA ex-
students' club which gave performances on Sunday nights. It
was about a psychiatrist—I'd never heard of one before—and
I was asked to take over the role of the patient at short notice
from the brilliant Meggie Albanesi, who had been taken ill. I
was in an all-star cast with dear Athene Seyler, Ian Swinley,
and Arthur Pusey, who was so beautiful I forgot my words
every time he kissed me.

I am sure that Sir Kenneth wanted to give me a second
chance to come to the notice of agents and managers. I did get
very good reviews, and two fan letters—one from Miles
Malleson and one from the producer at the Liverpool Repertory. Unfortunately, his new season was just starting and was
already fully cast.

Three years later, when I was again out of work, Sir Kenneth
introduced me to J. B. Fagan, and I was allowed to read
several parts in an audition for the Oxford Playhouse Repertory. I got that engagement, and was in the first play there,
Shaw's *Heartbreak House*.

Edward, Prince of Wales, opened the Malet Street Theatre
in the summer of 1921. He was bronzed from a trip abroad, and

golden blond. He sat in a huge chair that looked much too big for him and fidgeted and blushed, while we three medallists giggled and squealed in the wings, waiting to go out, curtsey, and receive our awards. Imagine our embarrassment when we discovered that the Prince's equerry was standing very close to us and had overheard all our silly remarks!

The Prince then watched a play enacted by the contemporary students, followed by a most exciting first performance of Sir James Barrie's *Shall We Join the Ladies?*, with Gerald du Maurier, Lady Tree and Irene Vanbrugh in the cast.

In conclusion: why do people think you cannot be *taught* to act? There are two sides to every art: technique and feeling. Technique you can never learn enough about. Ballet dancers, musicians, singers constantly find new teachers after they have become great stars. Technique in acting, I think, is ninety per cent control of the feeling—not faking it, but controlling it with the utmost firmness, as I was taught by such experts as Moffat Johnson, Helen Haye and Sybil Thorndike.

You *can* learn technique. But only life can teach you how to feel.

Robert Morley

Robert Morley was born at Semley in Wiltshire in 1908, and attended the Royal Academy of Dramatic Art 1926–28. Originally intended for a diplomatic career—or so he always thought—he in fact made his first stage appearance at the Hippodrome in Margate two days after his 20th birthday, playing in Dr Syn. His first London appearance came 18 months later as a pirate in Treasure Island; then followed a season at Cambridge, Shakespeare tours with Frank Benson, and the founding (with Peter Bull in 1935) of the Perranporth Repertory Theatre in Cornwall, believed to be the only one for which hampers of food for the cast were delivered by Fortnum & Mason. In 1936 he made his name in Oscar Wilde in London and New York, a performance which led to his MGM film debut as Louis XVI opposite Norma Shearer and Tyrone Power in Marie Antoinette.

Since then there have been nearly a hundred other films, including Major Barbara (1940), An Outcast of the Islands (1951), The African Queen (1952), The Doctor's Dilemma (1959), Oscar Wilde (1960), Those Magnificent Men in Their Flying Machines (1963), and most recently, Someone is Killing the Great Chefs of Europe.

On stage, his best-known appearances have been in his own plays, Edward My Son and Hippo Dancing (adapted from the French), as well as The Man Who Came to Dinner (1941), The First Gentleman (1945), The Little Hut (1950), A Majority of One (1960), Halfway Up A Tree (1967), How the Other Half Loves (1970), and Banana Ridge (1976). He has also appeared in a one-man show, The Sound of Morley, and published an autobiography and two collections of short pieces. A regular contributor to Punch, Robert Morley was awarded the CBE in 1957.

O ver cocktails she bemoaned Milton Keynes. She had spent the afternoon there doing things for the County. Not that there was anything to be done for Milton Keynes itself; far too many houses too close together and an absence apparently of skilled labour. 'All these planners,' she lamented, 'such a botch, it's difficult to forgive what they have done to the Whaddon Chase Country. I stay on but my son has given up completely, moved to the Quorn.'

'I understand exactly how you must feel,' I told her. 'I myself have spent the afternoon revisiting happy hunting grounds to find them sadly changed.'

'You still ride?' she asked, incredulous.

I never rode, but what is even more surprising, at my age, I still act. I had spent the afternoon at the Royal Academy of Dramatic Art where fifty years ago an eager child of nineteen first showed his paces to an astonished selection committee, a member of which, I have always affirmed, was the late Gerald du Maurier. Alas, the files—one has now to call them archives —do not support my claim. The examiners are listed as Kate Rourke and the Principal himself (in those days Kenneth, later to become Sir Kenneth, Barnes).

Sir Kenneth was the brother of the Vanbrugh girls, Irene and Violet, the equivalent in those days of our own Dame Wendy Hiller and Dame Peggy Ashcroft. Father, who knew everyone slightly but no one quite enough, provided a letter to Irene, who seemed surprised to receive it at my hands. It dealt at some length, I gathered, with the difficulty of finding a suitable occupation for a young gentleman without private means or much expectation of inheriting any. It went on to beg her intercession with her brother that a place might be found at the opening of the autumn term. 'I don't think,' she opined, having read the missive, 'that there is likely to be a problem, just go round to RADA and ask for the enrolment form. They'll tell you when you have to audition and I am sure they'll be delighted to have you as a student, dear boy.' Irene was famous not only as a comedienne but also for her good manners.

A study of the candidates' list on which my name appears proved her correct in her surmise. In those days few indeed were ever turned away, and they were invariably girls. Against a list of forty or so candidates the word 'no' appears only three times. It was easier in those days, I remarked to Mr O'Donoghue, the present registrar, who had received me most warmly at tea time, proferring chocolate biscuits and the relevant files for my consumption.

'It had to be,' he replied. 'In those days the Academy was not independently wealthy as it is today, thanks to the Shaw Bequests, and Kenneth had to see it paid its way. The number of students was roughly eight times what it is today. Of course, the whole place was a great deal smaller. We rebuilt after the bomb.'

Crunching the biscuits, I recalled for him the magic of Bernard Shaw's first lecture which I was privileged to attend. I can see him now, striding onto the small stage, removing his hat and beginning to unbutton his overcoat. 'I want you to watch carefully,' he told us, 'while Bernard Shaw, the great Bernard Shaw, takes off his coat.' In point of fact, although I never knew it at the time, Shaw's participation in the life of the Academy had been constant since its foundation. An active member of the Council, there are many Minutes of his suggestions as to how the school should be run in the early days. Once he suggested that students should be made to stand on the stage and read a page of the French telephone directory aloud so as to get a grasp of Gallic pronounciation. Another time he thought that the students should perform a play in a completely empty West End theatre–empty, that is, save for the Council, who would watch from the top of the gallery. I have written elsewhere of my adoration of Saint Bernard who awakened me at the age of thirteen from the stupor and despair of adolescence, and during a performance of *The Doctor's Dilemma* made me realize there was to be no life for me thereafter save in the theatre. Now he was in the same room granting a semi-private audience.

What astonished me most in those early days at the Academy was the discovery that actors and actresses like Norman Page, Herbert Ross, Helen Haye, Rosina Phillipi, Dorothy Green were alive and well and visiting Gower Street. I don't know exactly how I expected people who acted would look or behave, but I was unprepared to find them no different in appearance and manner from men who pushed pens or flogged stocks and shares. They weren't even so very different from my own uncles and aunts, though none of the latter included a member of the 'Profession' among their acquaintances, and if they ever spoke of or visited the theatre took a certain pride in never being able accurately to record the impressions gained. Thus they would remark that the other night someone had taken them—they never ventured on their own—to that theatre in the Haymarket where there was quite an amusing piece written by that fellow with the double-barrelled name, and acted by the chap who used to play Shakespeare. 'I tell you who was in it as well, that short comedienne who used to be married to Cosmo Gordon Lennox, didn't she?' They would look round, feigning ignorance, and someone would helpfully change the subject. No one cared to state unequivocally that St John Irvine had written *The Second Mrs Fraser* and that Harry Ainley and Marie Tempest were its stars. Inexplicably,

the only name they never seemed to forget was Matheson
Lang's.

My father was the exception. He actually played auction
bridge with Charles Hawtrey, and once took me behind the
scenes to see Fred Neilson-Terry when he visited Folkestone,
and insisted on my actually perching on the chair he had
recently vacated as the Scarlet Pimpernel himself. Neither
Mr Terry nor I thought it a very good idea at the time. At
the age of six I don't think it occurred to me that the star was
anxious to be off home for his tea and that the costume he was
wearing would soon be changed for something a good deal more
casual. Of course, I didn't expect the staff at the Academy to
be in costume when I first set eyes on them, but then I don't
think it occurred to me they would be in flannels and sports
coats either.

Norman Page, who was more or less second-in-command to
Kenneth Barnes, was currently playing in *Marigold* at the
Kingsway Theatre. The piece had already been performed for
nearly a year, which was something of a phenomenon in those
days, and Mr Page had the reputation of having been the best
pantomime cat within living memory, and had only recently
shed his skin forever after being pushed by a young admirer off
his perch on the dress circle rail and falling heavily into the
stalls beneath—without, luckily, causing much damage, except
to himself and a number of tea trays. He was the kindest of
men, and seldom took acting seriously, his interest constantly
caught and often sustained at least for a term by a more than
usually pretty student. At the first class he conducted with the
new intake, he always enquired which of his charges had
decided on a stage career against the express wishes and advice
of their parents. Quite untruthfully my arm shot up. I was
anxious to impress him with my singleness of purpose and
determination, but it was a girl child in the front who caught
and held his attention, and he closely questioned her as to
whether she had actually run away from home or whether her
parents were supporting her at the YWCA. It was surprising

how many of the class seemed to have braved parental disapproval, but in those days to have a son or daughter on the
stage was not—as it is now—a matter for congratulation. A
couple of years ago on the Isle of Wight, a proud father showed
me a record sleeve featuring his nubile daughter, completely
nude, though admittedly photographed from behind. He was
justly proud of the number of records which she had sold for
the group of which she was not as yet a member. Such an
attitude would have been unthinkable in my early days, even
on the Isle of Wight, but then of course no one had thought of
record sleeves.

But if parents were different then, so were we students. A
great many of us were hell-bent not on dedication so much as
fornication. Here I must make clear that I am speaking
principally of members of my own sex, who were happily
outnumbered by the girls in the ratio of seven or eight to one.
That meant not only that most of us young pashas were never
again to have it so good on or off stage, but that we enjoyed
the inestimable benefit of being allowed to play Hamlet—or
even, in my own case, Shylock—from start to finish supported
by a constantly changing Juliet or Portia. There would come a
moment during the performance when one Juliet would
disentangle herself from Romeo's embrace, demurely leave
the stage, and be instantly replaced by another hopeful
debutante. It made for a certain amount of confusion but must
have often proved a relief to Sir Kenneth, who made it a point
of honour to watch every single performance given under his
roof. It would be difficult to pay sufficient tribute to his sense
of dedication and his infinite compassion and patience, and it
proved quite impossible when he came to retire to find another
who was prepared to undergo such sustained and prolonged
torture. But while I was there Sir Kenneth still ruled, and on
the memorable occasion of my own Shylock, he appeared
suddenly in front of the tabs to suppress a near riot among my
fellow students, who had found my acting with Tubal so
hilarious that they screamed and demanded an encore. Sir

Kenneth quelled them with a short speech. 'Now,' he said, 'let us all remember: fair is fair', and indicated the performance was to continue. I have never to this day understood why I was considered so funny as Shylock; indeed, once or twice I have been tempted to play the part again just to find out the cause. Once, after a particularly fine dinner, Peter Hall, who was still at Stratford, urged me to join his company in any role I fancied. 'I might do Shylock,' I told him, and he promised to ring in the morning. It was just unfortunate my 'phone happened to have been out of order.

I enquired of Mr O'Donoghue whether the legend of my performance still persisted, but he thought not. 'You were marked "Above Average" that term,' he told me, pushing forward the relevant document. Together we read the names of my contemporaries, about whose subsequent careers I was a mine of misinformation; believing for instance, that the late and much loved Joan Harben had married a poet. Mr O'Donoghue pointed out that *Who's Who* listed her as having married Clive Morton, another dear friend, who died last year, alas. Far too many of my contemporaries seem to have done just that, but we were back happily in the land of the living with Jean Anderson, the ever-ailing but fortunately never actually succumbing Mother of that popular television series, *The Brothers*.

I fell to wondering about Alan Webb, whom I had seen the night before in a revival of *The Seagull* on the box. 'Was he here with you?' asked the Registrar. 'He was here before me, I think,' I told him, 'but no doubt the records don't go back that far.' 'On the contrary,' he assured me, 'I was looking up Athene Seyler who popped in the other day. She was here in 1908, when any performance the students gave took place in the front drawing-room—except, of course, for the Public Show.'

The Public Show, now discontinued, was The Event of our two-year course—the day, as the title suggests, when we appeared in public in a real West End Theatre (in my day the

St James's), and were reviewed by professional critics in the daily press. The Academy itself awarded Gold, Silver and Bronze Medals to the outstanding students. Reading the roll of honour hung in the entrance hall and signed not only by all the fortunate recipients but also by Dame Madge Kendal herself, who penned the immortal advice 'To Your Own Self Be True' in the firm hand associated with her strict code of morals and deportment, one is surprised at how often the judges guessed right. The list is impressive: Charles Laughton, Robert Shaw, Robert Atkins, Athene Seyler, Meggie Albanesi, Alan Badel, Sian Phillips, Gemma Jones. Indeed, only in one instance was potential not apparently spotted. I myself was sent for by the Administrator at the end of my first year and questioned closely as to whether I had private means to sustain a further year in the direction of what Kenneth obviously regarded as—but was too polite actually to designate—a suicidal course. Whenever I met him subsequently and he thought I was about to repeat the tale, he begged me to desist on the grounds that I had not heard him correctly.

Besides the medals and certificates to be won annually there was a feast of other prizes and awards, usually bearing the name of the donor (sometimes still extant but more often deceased) who had bequeathed a sum sufficient to keep his name alive by the annual distribution of largesse, which in those days usually amounted to about five guineas. There was the Kenneth Kent Award for Attack in Acting, The Hamen Clark Award for Diction in Relation to Dialect, Mrs Willard's Prize for Spontaneous Laughter, and V. C. Buckley's Prize for the Wearing of Clothes Period or Modern. None of us in my time was a dedicated pot hunter, but we were encouraged by the staff to enter these gladiatorial contests if only that they might have a further insight into our failings in the field, for instance, of mime or fencing. No subject bored me more than that of the study of the foil and I seldom attended the great Monsieur Bertram's celebrated classes which, like the dance classes, I gave as wide a berth as was allowable, and there was a good deal of flexibility in the regulations which ordained how many appearances one should put in each term. I was an ungraceful youth and I fear no amount of thrust, parry and tiptoe would have made me otherwise. In any case, I never tried. At almost my first session at the dancing class I was singled out as the square boy at the back and made to stand in front of my comrades on the grounds that I had most to learn. I never returned.

Imagine my delight, therefore, when discovering—as I have already boasted—that I was marked 'above average' in my first term. Above average, indeed! I should hope so. But who were the others? In 1926 when I first came on the scene the Academy was still recovering from Charles Laughton, who was to do for Gower Street what John Osborne was later to achieve for Sloane Square. He changed the image. Regarded as unlikely material when he first arrived, with his Yorkshire accent and flying yellow mackintosh, he carried all before him, including his enormous frame, won every prize, caught every judge's eye, and almost immediately after leaving gave—in what was then the fringe theatre at Kew—the first performance of *The Government Inspector* London had seen for years.

I was no Laughton, although in bulk and general untidiness of costume I bore perhaps a fleeting resemblance, but Laughton heartened us fatties and the regional types who, by the nature of the Academy, were in those days still regarded rather as second-class citizens. If Kenneth Barnes was to run the Academy at even the smallest margin of profit he had perforce to run it first and foremost as a charm school. Mothers who hadn't wanted to put their daughters on the stage were much more likely to continue paying the fees if they noticed a distinct improvement in their child's posture and appearance, in the way she spoke and dressed and brushed her hair. A year at the Academy could often do wonders in turning a dumpy duck into an acceptable cygnet. For the men, of course, no such transformation was possible—or, indeed, thought desirable— but some parents remained hopeful that at the end of two years their sons would change direction and consider a more serious and gainful career. Indeed, had all four hundred or so of the student body who crowded the classrooms been inspired by the staff with unwavering purpose and devotion to its temporary vocation the profession would have been even more hopelessly crowded than it is today. Many of us fell by the roadside, or more properly thumbed a lift to town by way of early marriage or the acceptance of a job in our father's business; but a surprising number of my year remained on the stage to tell the tale—or enable me to do so for Mr O'Donoghue, who passed me list after list of their half-forgotten names.

Dorothy Dunkels, along with a girl called Majorie Playfair, and Plum Warner's daughter Betty, were the three great beauties of our day. Miss Playfair had the prettiest legs imaginable and she would sit swinging them on the dresser of the canteen to the hopeless admiration of most of the fellows and indeed some of the staff. Betty Warner had the most beautiful red hair, and Dorothy Dunkels was teacher's pet—at least where Miss Sevening was concerned. Miss Sevening was the formidable power behind and indeed on the scenes. It was generally admitted that it was she who ran the show. She was Baroness Falkender to Barnes's Harold Wilson. She kept things moving, knew what was going on, and on occasions stopped the rot. I suppose what she liked about Dorothy Dunkels was that she was nearly, if not quite, as elegant as herself. Much to our surprise Dorothy didn't carry all before her on the day. I am not certain she even won a prize, but I remember her at the Strand Theatre later giving a memorable performance as a manicurist in one of Arthur Macrae's plays and looking the same cool and lovely child she had when she sat beside Majorie but didn't swing her legs.

'You knew, of course,' I told O'Donoghue, 'that Grizel Niven was David Niven's sister and became a sculptress and that Inagret Giffard married Laurence Van Der Post and that Cheatle committed suicide and so did Sandford who won the Gold.' 'I knew about Sandford,' he told me, 'Barnes wrote

RIP after his name.' 'I don't know what happened to Elizabeth Thynne,' I said, and O'Donoghue told me Barnes had written RIP after her name as well.

Bruno Barnabe is still going and so is Brian Oulton and, of course, Jean Anderson and Hugh Moxey. I caught him on television only the other day. Esther Thomson, now she married Komisarjevsky or was it Claude Rains? I'm pretty sure it was Rains not Komisarjevsky. Come and seduce me, we used to call him.

Carol Hahn married Llewellyn Rees who became Secretary of Equity but then afterwards she married Giles Playfair, whose father Sir Nigel ran the Lyric Theatre, Hammersmith. 'There is a Carol Hahn Memorial Award,' O'Donoghue told me, 'she was American.'

'They were married straight from the Academy, I rather think,' I told him. 'I gave her away, at any rate Llewellyn was *my* best man when I married. I'm afraid it's all getting a trifle blurred. Did you know,' I asked, surer of my ground, 'that Wallace Finlayson was really Wallace Douglas, Robert Douglas's brother? Robert stepped straight into *Many Waters* as the Jeune Premier and then went into films and still produces them for television. Or that André Van Gysegem married Jean Forbes-Robertson. Curigwen Lewis, now she *did* marry a poet.'

'Andrew Cruickshank,' he reproved me gently.

'Joan Hickson is still going strong,' I came back at him. 'Did you see her in the Ayckbourn play?'

'*Bedroom Farce*,' he countered.

I began to understand my aunts and uncles all those years ago. Perhaps it wasn't pretence, forgetting the names.

I was on surer ground where the staff were concerned. 'Miss Elsie Chester had one leg and a crutch she used to throw at us when she couldn't bear it any longer. Helen Haye always acted Grand Duchesses clutching cambric handkerchiefs. A great teacher. Once, after I had been particularly terrible in *The Last of Mrs Cheyney*, she firmly opened a copy of the *Evening*

Standard Racing Edition. 'I am unlikely,' she remarked, not unkindly, 'to find a winner in this class. We must try Sandown Park.'

There was the great Rosina Phillipi—retired, I think, by this time—who taught breath control. You were expected to do Mark Antony's speech about Brutus not bringing chariots to Rome in three breaths. For years afterwards I used to test myself. Now if I manage a length underwater in the pool I am content.

All the staff had their favourite plays. Elsie Chester's was Galsworthy's *The Silver Box*. Herbert Ross, married to Helen Haye, stuck more or less to *Tilly of Bloomsbury*. Norman Page was devoted to one by Dunsany about a Pierrot. Then there was an elocution teacher, or more properly a voice production coach, who made you stand at the end of the room and bounce final consonants off the opposite wall. Hop Poles Unchecked Desire. 'I still do it.'

'Do what?'

'Sound the final consonant. None of the young do; that's why I can't hear them, that and because I am a bit deaf.'

'Would you like,' he said, 'to go and see the Young People?'

'I'd quite like to go and see the old place.'

Like Milton Keynes, it had sadly changed. The canteen is upstairs and the basement where it used to be is now a small theatre. It was as if I had never seen the place before. I suppose in a way I hadn't. Once, when I was about to go into the old theatre, I leant heavily against a door which gave way and I found myself in the disused box office. Quick as a flash I opened up for business. 'It's half a crown now for each parent,' I told my fellow students as they streamed past. Some of them even gave me their half-crowns. When I had counted up, I slipped inside the auditorium. I couldn't hear the play because of the whispered protests of those who had paid and the gleeful pleasure of those who hadn't. Barnes sent for me later and confiscated the loot for the Building Fund—what was left of it. In those days half a crown went a long way. You could eat at

Bertorelli's in Percy Street on newspapers for tenpence. A huge bowl of spaghetti and an apple dumpling. Enough for growing boys and girls.

The grown boys and girls were in the basement preparing to rehearse an extemporization, the sort of thing they do in Hampstead. 'At least they don't have to learn the lines,' I said to the rather severe young woman who seemed to be in charge. 'Indeed they do,' she told me, 'once we've decided on the script.' 'Have you decided on this one?' 'Not yet.' 'Will it be a happy piece?' I asked. 'Not particularly,' she said. 'It's about a group of students and their problems. I hope it will be a true picture.' I told her I hoped so too, and climbed the stairs to retrieve my hat and coat. 'What about her,' I asked, 'is she a permanent member of your staff?' 'Visiting,' O'Donoghue assured me, 'after this she is off to the Crucible at Sheffield to stage the same sort of exercise.' 'She is leading them down a path only the critics will follow,' I told him sagely.

There was one chocolate biscuit left on the plate. I munched it all the way to the bus stop. Age has its compensations, but then I always had a sweet tooth.

Lilli Palmer

Lilli Palmer was born in Austria and studied at the Ilka Grüning School of Acting, Berlin. Her first stage appearance in Berlin was in 1932, and she subsequently played in repertory companies and appeared in cabaret before coming to London in 1935 to act in films. She made her first appearance on the London stage in 1938 in The Road to Gandahar, *and several other West End plays followed. She made her New York debut in 1949 in* My Name is Aquilon, *followed by* Caesar and Cleopatra. *Other stage successes have been* Bell, Book and Candle, Venus Observed, The Love of Four Colonels, *and* Suite in Three Keys.

Among her many films are Thunder Rock, The Four Poster, Is Anna Anderson Anastasia?, Conspiracy of Hearts, The Pleasure of His Company, The Counterfeit Traitor, Operation Crossbow, Hard Contract, The Marquis de Sade. *She was recently seen in the television series* The Zoo Gang, *and is currently filming* The Boys from Brazil.

Miss Palmer is married to Carlos Thompson and lives in Switzerland.

J began to attend a drama school when I was fifteen, while still at school studying for my baccalauréat. I wanted to be an actress; my father wanted me to be a doctor, and insisted that I finish my formal schooling and get my high school diploma. I decided to do both at the same time. This double life was a little ambitious, but very good training for later on. Thus in the morning I went to high school, and in the afternoon I rushed off to the then most select school for young actors and actresses, an academy run by two famous elderly actresses—the German equivalent of, say, Dame Edith Evans and Dame Sybil Thorndike.

These two ladies lived together and every two years selected twelve boys and twelve girls from among many hopeful young aspirants, and gave them a two-year training. Each pupil had a personal one-hour lesson every day during which the others watched and somebody gave cues, and you learned as much from the lessons of others, as you did from your own individual tuition.

For the first six months we did nothing but voice exercises and elocution; but after that we began to play small parts and graduated onto bigger roles. And after two years had passed we gave a public performance which was attended by all the producers and directors of the German repertory companies. We finished products of this two-year training course each performed two contrasting roles—a serious one and a light one, usually, in order to display our versatility—and before the evening was out all twenty-four of us could expect to be engaged by the various repertory companies. This is the best way to begin a career in the theatre, of course.

I was engaged by the Darmstadt State Theatre, one of the best-known repertory companies in Germany at that time. There I stayed for a year, until my career in Germany was abruptly terminated in 1933, soon after Hitler came to power, and I left for England. Although just a raw beginner, trying to find my way around, I fancied I knew all there was to know, that I was an accomplished actress ready for anything, even film roles. I coasted along on what I thought I knew, which in reality was very little. My acting technique was extremely basic—though I was sincere. I thought sincerity was very important. If I was called upon to act in a happy scene, well, then, I laughed a lot; and if it was a sad scene, well, then, I tried to cry. But I really hadn't a clue what the craft of acting, what the *art* really consisted of. And yet, by some marvellous luck— or perhaps it was because I didn't photograph too badly—I came under contract to a film company called Gaumont-British, and I played leading roles. Then one day I met Beate Moissi, the daughter of Alexander Moissi who was a very famous German actor. This woman, who had been brought up among the theatrical elite, said to me, 'Listen, I saw you yesterday on the screen in that new film of yours, and I want to tell you that you are *so* bad—you even manage to look old, and at twenty that's quite a feat.'

I was aghast.

She continued, 'I'm not saying this to annoy you, but so that you may learn. I happen to know someone here in London who could teach you—if you're very lucky she might take you on.'

Now, I shall cut this story short because you don't really want to know about my heart-searchings and about my anger and my fury because I thought I was a leading lady already and I was not doing too badly, and I was twenty years old and I was very pretty. Something inside me whispered that maybe I wasn't that hot and maybe I wasn't that pretty and maybe I wasn't that good. Maybe I ought to learn. The woman that Beate Moissi mentioned was called Elsa Schreiber, and the very next day when I appeared before her with a film script, she overlooked my pretentions and my silly behaviour as a screen diva and began to work with me. And she worked with me very evening after I had finished at the studios. Instead of going home, I used to rush to her house where she would have something nourishing ready for me—usually spinach, because she was a health fanatic—and then, with my script on her lap, we started to work on my role. She taught me the most elementary rules of the game, rules which I didn't even know existed. The very first thing she said to me, shaking her head at the way I uttered the very first line, was: 'Don't show me your talent, please.' I was amazed—I felt that I was *paid* to show my talent. I had to learn that this was the very last thing I should do— that I should *hide* my talent. I had to learn that a sad scene can be infinitely sadder if it is played with a smile on your face, and that in a 'happy' scene the last thing I should do was laugh. I had to learn that if I went to a window on stage and opened it and the line was: 'Oh what a beautiful morning— and how brightly the sun is shining!' I should not say it as I was used to doing as gay as a lark. That would be too coy for words, and would alienate the audience. Elsa taught me that if ever I had two such dreadful lines to say, then I would just have to take the sting out of them by saying them absolutely plainly, and only then would the audience believe me.

Well, when you're twenty years old and fairly addle-pated, and also very conceited, it takes quite a long time for such lessons to sink in. Because I was defending my primitive ideas of acting and she was trying to din into me certain basic rules, we fought a battle—a battle royal. I am amazed now at her patience and the way she put up with my pretentions and my bad manners. But eventually I caught on and began to understand what she was trying to teach me, and I began to trust her.

In the meantime I was getting on with my stage career, and I appeared for the first time on the London stage in a terrible play called *The Road to Gandahar*. Needless to say, when the script was sent to me I was so elated and so pleased—I thought it was the greatest play in the world and that my role in it was the greatest role ever. When I showed it to Elsa she said, 'It's a terrible play—and yours is certainly a long role.' That was all she said. But she coached me so well that I got the first really excellent notices of my life. After that I worked with her every single day for the next three years.

Just before the war, Elsa left London with her husband to go to Hollywood. I felt that it was good for me not to be able to turn to her for help, that it was time to stand on my own feet. However, when my first husband (Rex Harrison) and I arrived in Hollywood after the war and I had my first screen test for the leading role opposite Gary Cooper in *Cloak and Dagger*, I naturally hot-footed it to Elsa to work on the test with her. And I got the part. Later, when I was rehearsing my first play on Broadway, she came once again to my rescue, and I got good notices in an otherwise disastrous production.

Elsa became a legend in the American theatre. Some of the greatest names in show business have worked with her, and for some of them she has literally been the making of their careers. Rex was no mean actor—indeed, he was already considered the best English high comedy actor—yet, when he played his first character role as the king in *Anna and the King of Siam* (it was also his first Hollywood role), Elsa coached him in every detail. After that he worked with her on three or four other films. I mention this only to show what a very special and extraordinary woman she is. I won't list all the other actors whom she has worked with because, strangely, I have found them very reticent about the help she has given them. I never was; I don't think I lose any prestige by admitting that I learnt a great deal from someone. Elsa Schreiber taught me my business, my trade; even more than that, she moulded me as a person. From her I understood that one can even learn charm—'You haven't got any,' she used to say to me. 'You behave like a schoolmistress, but you can learn.'

Eventually, of course, the time had to come when Elsa was not available. I was to play in *Caesar and Cleopatra* on Broadway, and Elsa could not leave Hollywood. Rex told me, 'It's just as well—now you'll just have to rely on yourself—even if it is a big part like this one.' I worked on Cleopatra on my own, thinking hard about what Elsa would have done with every single sentence. She would have said, 'Try saying it the other way round. Try it upside down. Try it with the opposite sense. See if that works. Think. *Think*.' I am happy to say it was a huge success, something I love to think back on.

I never worked with Elsa Schreiber again—for no better reason than that I thought I was now emancipated and should develop alone. I'm often asked by aspiring young actors and actresses, 'What would you recommend me to do, where should I go to learn?' I never know quite what to answer, because it's very risky to recommend to others something that has worked so well for oneself. If pressed, I have to say that if I were eighteen again I would do the same. If I couldn't go to a genius like Elsa, I would go to a great actress of an older vintage, and I would beg her to train me. I would go there three times a week. For me, that would be preferable to going to a drama school, but others might find the company of fellow students a more stimulating way to learn.

Dulcie Gray

Dulcie Gray was born in Kuala Lumpur, Malaysia. Educated from the ages of $3\frac{1}{2}$–14 in England, she returned to Malaysia and at 16 became an assistant teacher at a boarding school. Not long afterwards she worked her passage to England on a cargo boat, arriving with £10, won a scholarship to a painting school, then to the Webber-Douglas, where she met her husband-to-be, Michael Denison.

Her first London part was Alexandra in The Little Foxes *in 1942. She made her name in* Brighton Rock *in 1943, and was at once put under a film contract. She made a great many films, including* They Were Sisters, A Man About the House, Mine Own Executioner, *etc., on her own, and* My Brother Jonathan, The Glass Mountain, The Franchise Affair *and several others with her husband. She has played 37 times in the West End, 22 times with Michael Denison, and successes include* Queen Elizabeth Slept Here, The Four Poster, Candida, Where Angels Fear To Tread, An Ideal Husband, At the End of the Day, *and, most recently,* A Murder is Announced.

Miss Gray has published a play, 17 crime novels, a book of short stories, and, with her husband, An Actor and His World. *She has had 7 radio plays performed and many short horror stories published in anthologies. She has been Vice President of the British Butterfly Conservation Society for 10 years, and her book* Butterflies on My Mind *will be published in 1978.*

For the two years that I was at drama school, I allowed myself 6d (2½p) a day for food, so for most of the time I didn't feel very well, but I was happy. Today more than seventy per cent of the students are in receipt of county grants. At that time grants did not exist, so I had to finance myself through the course.

I had already worked my passage to England from Malaya on a cargo boat, looking after a child of two. I had then won a scholarship to a painting school run by Amédée Ozenfant, the purist painter who had taught Léger some years before in Paris. By mutual agreement it was felt that the scholarship offered to me by the Webber-Douglas Academy of Dramatic Art might be more productive; a scholarship which, in fact, was never awarded, since Barbara Mullen had also been given one, and there was only one on offer. The fees were £15 per term for me, as a special concession to my lost scholarship (the other students paid £18); this made things quite tough, but I made money from nude modelling and from teaching English to a Spanish girl and an Italian girl. (As I knew no Spanish or Italian, the rate for the job wasn't high.) I sold my surrealist pictures, and walked a dog for one of the members of staff for five shillings a week.

The Webber-Douglas was chiefly known at that time as a singing school, although drama was becoming increasingly important in the curriculum. Mr Webber, one of the co-principals, who looked like a rosy-cheeked, Beatrix Potter dormouse, was the musical director, and Madame Enriqueta Crichton staged the opera performances. She was tall, mysterious, languid and magnificent. Mr Johnstone Douglas, the other co-principal, was quiet, remote and charming. He taught singing as he himself had been taught by the celebrated singer Jean de Reske. 'J.D.', as we all called him, had had a tremendous success in *The Immortal Hour*, and was therefore greatly respected. He was also an astute business man, as I later had good cause to discover.

The drama side was headed by Ellen O'Malley, a great lady of the theatre. At the peak of her stage career she had been much admired by George Bernard Shaw—in fact she had played many of his great roles under his personal direction. Ellie Dunn, the young heroine of *Heartbreak House*, had been especially written for her, but by the time it was produced in 1921 it had been on the stocks for eight years, and she was too old for it. The critics screamed with rage at the casting, but Shaw defended her spiritedly, writing to St John Ervine, 'I did not cast Ellen for Ellie Dunn—I wrote it for her, and it fits her like a glove!'

When I first met Ellen she must have been in her sixties. She was thick-set and very lame, with small, blue, short-sighted eyes, a vague—not to say distracted—manner, a beautiful, booming voice, and the most elusive pair of steel-rimmed spectacles imaginable. Hours of everyone's time were spent in searching for them. She was a good-tempered, enchanting woman, and a marvellous teacher. I had enormous affection for her. In 1960, when Michael Denison (my husband) and I managed to bring Shaw back to the West End (it was then believed that he was box-office poison) with a successful revival of *Candida* at the Piccadilly Theatre, and later at Wyndham's, it was delightful to know that Ellen approved of what we had done, and the way we were trying to do it.

Susan Richmond, a meticulous theorist, was another teacher.

She had written a very useful little book on the technique of acting, and though for me her almost niggling precision was not sympathetic, she was a good antidote to the breadth and imaginativeness of Ellen O'Malley's methods. Molly Terraine, who afterwards became head of J. Arthur Rank's 'Charm School' for film starlets, was the only teacher allowed to do a whole play a term, instead of the usual practice of handling only one act, and thus was particularly helpful.

And there was Alison Leggatt. At that time she was a glamorous young leading lady, and was actually acting with Noël Coward and Gertrude Lawrence in *Tonight at 8.30* in the West End in the evenings, while teaching us during the day, so the stardust hung thick about her. She turned me from an amateur in outlook into a professional. Today she is a brilliant character actress.

Then, as now, the Webber-Douglas was situated in Clareville Grove, just off the Gloucester Road. Then, as now, the pretty little Chanticleer Theatre was its centre. A low wall still runs in front of the school, and this, in my time, was the meeting place for friends and gossip on fine days. There we would discuss our futures as passionately as though there were no threat of war ahead, as though acting were the only worthwhile activity on earth.

Photographs of former students who had made the grade— among them Stewart Granger, Renée Asherson and Victoria Hopper— looked down encouragingly at us from the walls of the large basement room where I had auditioned for entry before 'J.D.', Molly Terraine, and the school secretary, Carina Thurburn, declaiming 'The quality of mercy is not strained'. (When asked why I had chosen that particular speech, I explained that it was a direct appeal to them, and they laughed.) In the basement we did exercises under the supervision of a big, lazy woman who was so bored with having to teach us that she sometimes nodded off to sleep while drearily counting, 'One, two, three, four . . .' Since I was having to pay for my training, this annoyed me so intensely that one day I ran to the piano and banged out 'God send you back to me' very loudly, in march time, which not only woke her but started us doing exercises to music for the rest of my time there. It was a great improvement.

On another, dreadful, occasion when we were doing something called 'stage training' with that same lazy woman—it meant being given a word or a scene and being asked to improvise, and took place in the theatre—a sad and hideous girl with no talent, a fierce black moustache, and no self-confidence, who had been waiting, scared to death, for her turn to come on stage, made a terrified entrance and wet her pants in fright in a long, tremendous stream. We watched her, aghast, but the teacher, who as usual had her eyes shut, merely said as automatically as she said to every girl who came on stage, 'Very nice, dear. Now go back and do it all over again.' The girl left the school.

There was an attic room where we did fencing with a fencing master who disliked me so much because I was so bad at it that he literally used to hiss that my end-of-term report would be dreadful. Since my father was dead and my mother living in Singapore, this left me unmoved. There was a garage where we did speech training, learning poems like 'Horses on the Camargue' and 'Do you remember an inn, Miranda?', and other such pieces, and once a week we went by train to a large rehearsal room in Earl's Court where we did mime under the watchful eyes of Miss Mawer, handsome in a grey leotard, and a small tea-cosy of a woman who accompanied us on the piano.

Miss Mawer had a fixation about the French Revolution which unfortunately no one had seen fit to mention to me, and when on my first day, with me at the head of the column, she told us to mime it, and little Miss Tea-Cosy triumphantly lashed out 'The Marseillaise' on her small upright piano, I shambled eccentrically round the room as a toothless, leering old tricoteuse, only to find that the rest of the class were striding with starry eyes and heads held high towards an

everlastingly invigorating future. Miss Mawer was very angry
with me.

Holidays were something of a problem, but I had several
kind relations who put me up for short periods, and I also
found work. One job was to model for my Aunt Gemma's
sister, Mary McDowall, who with two friends had decided to
spend part of the summer painting at her house in Berkshire.
The three of them had been together at the Slade many years
before, and this was to be in the nature of a reunion. Unfortunately the years had changed them very considerably, and far
from being a happy reunion it was nearer a disaster, since they
never stopped quarrelling. For me, however, this discord had
its advantages, as during the times that I was modelling for
them they argued so fiercely that I never had to hold a position
for long. Even in the summer I felt the cold so intensely that I
had to secrete a hot water bottle under the rug I was lying on
or the chair I was sitting on, so I found the ladies' lack of
harmony all gain. My pay consisted of my railway fare, my keep
(mostly a diet of mushrooms which I had to pick myself, after
work), and £2 a week. While I was picking the mushrooms I
was accompanied by Patrick, a spaniel who was subject to
violent fits.

But these were nothing to the eccentricities of Timmy, the
dog I walked during the term, a fat and aging terrier who had
long since lost any desire for exercise, and who deeply resented
my intrusions into his life. Unhappily, I would peal the front
door bell, and immediately there would be a scuffling noise on
the other side of the door. Timmy was old, but he was no fool.
Though to all other visitors he accorded a vociferous welcome,
as soon as he heard me he made hell-for-leather for the grandfather clock in the hall, under which he hid. The maid scorn-
fully let me in, and I had to spend the next ten minutes coaxing
Timmy out from under the clock, and then putting him on his
lead. From then on, my discomfiture grew. He so disliked
walking that I had to tow him up the Gloucester Road and

into the park on his behind. I adore dogs, and this always worried me, as did the hostile looks and rude remarks from passing dog-lovers, convinced that I was a case for the RSPCA.

There were about seventy-five girls and six or seven men for most of the time I was at the Webber-Douglas. Today this is very different, with men outnumbering women. Since the school had to finance itself through fee-paying students, there was quite a high proportion of debutantes, whose parents regarded the place as a finishing school. One mother actually said that her daughter would never be allowed to go on the stage, but she hoped she would learn in the two years she was to be a pupil, 'the art of coming into a room without knocking over the furniture'. Another debutante, on being greeted by Molly Terraine as a 'poor little rich girl'—at which several of us laughed sycophantically—drawled, 'You've had your fun, Miss Whatsit, now I'll have mine. I'm going to ring Mummy to send the Rolls, and it might interest you to know that she hasn't yet paid the cheque for my course at this emporium.'

I suppose I should have resented the fact that so many of the pupils weren't going to take up the stage as a profession, but I didn't. Most of them were cheerful, decorative girls, and many of them were very kind. Seeing the sort of lunches I ate, they generously invited me to their homes, where they fed me and made more sociable and interesting an existence which might have made me feel rather homesick for the East.

One day as I was walking back to my one-room home off the Earl's Court Road with a friend called Melancie, it began to pour with rain. I had no mackintosh and had forgotten my umbrella, so Melancie suggested we go instead to her grand-parents' home, where she was living at the time, as it was nearer. It wasn't particularly near, as it was in Belgrave Square, but I happily agreed. When we arrived we were soaked to the skin. None of Melancie's clothes fitted me, and her grandparents, whom I had never met, were out, so she decided I must have some brandy in order not to catch pneumonia.

She found some, and went off to change for a dinner date, leaving me sitting on the rug by the drawing-room fire. I drank the brandy, which went straight to my head, and when her grandfather returned home he found me fast asleep on the rug, clutching a bottle of his best brandy. He kindly let me stay there until I had slept it off, and then paid for a taxi to take me home.

Having so many debutantes did sometimes get on 'J.D.'"s nerves, especially in the summer when 'the Season' was at its height. Day after day, with the flimsiest of excuses, some of them would fail to turn up for work. At last he decided to make an example of them, and put up a notice on the board deploring their behaviour, and requesting certain of the worst offenders, whom he named, to write down their precise reasons for being absent so often. One girl, who had been absent no fewer than thirty times, wrote in a round, childish hand, 'Mummy says I had a headache' beside each of the dates in question.

At the beginning of my second term something happened to change my life. Michael came to the school as a student. At first I didn't take to him much. He was reserved and shy, and tremendously good-looking, which made me mistake his shyness for conceit. Some friends of his knew one of my uncles, who had asked me to look out for him and 'be nice to him'. With such a disproportionate number of women, he didn't need much looking after, and though the men got to know all the women students very well, since they acted in all the plays, we didn't see all that much of them.

I had a small and very fluctuating account with the Hong Kong and Shanghai Bank, which at that time had only one branch in London, in Gracechurch Street. I suddenly received a communication, written in pencil, which told me tersely that I was the proud possessor of an overdraft of six shillings and sevenpence. The Manager said he would like me to explain. There was little to explain: I had gone to them in the first place because it had been the bank my father used in Malaya, and now I had no money left. Michael had a car, so I asked him to drive me there. This he very kindly did, and in spite of the circumstances—which after all weren't particularly worrying as I was always very near the breadline in those days—we had a hilarious drive. I found him a delightful companion, and very funny. Very slowly, though friendship was certainly the first feeling we had for each other, we realized we were in love.

The first time we acted together was a test of character for me. The play was called *The King's Jewry*. Michael had an huge leading role. I had to play a bearded Jewish elder, with one line to say: 'It is now my part to listen.' As I had been listening for well over an hour by the time I spoke, and had also had to stand for the entire time, I didn't exactly revel in the proceedings, but the fact that it was Michael who was doing all the talking made a considerable difference.

Of the other students of my generation, very few have made names for themselves, probably because we were so soon to be plunged into war. I have mentioned Barbara Mullen, who from the start showed that she could act, and had, I believe, already earned her living as a child dancer before coming to drama school. There was also Rachel Gurney (the daughter of Irene Scharrer, the pianist), who is now well-known for her performances on television, including the series *Upstairs, Downstairs*. She was nearly two years ahead of me, and very much one of the stars of the establishment. She was then, as she is now, exquisitely beautiful, with an ethereal face and a lovely complexion. Helen Shingler, who played Madame Maigret in the Simenon series on television, was also outstanding, and Nicholas Meredith was just beginning to make a name for himself when he died, tragically young. Giles Cooper, a gentle creature with no talent as an actor but a remarkable gift for writing, was another friend. Years and years later Michael and I did one of our favourite plays at the St Martin's Theatre. It was called *Happy Family*, and was written by Giles. The critics loved it, but alas it made no money at the box-office.

Pamela Hulbert, the only daughter of Jack Hulbert and

Cicely Courtneidge, was another of the pupils. She was a dear, friendly creature with a splendid sense of humour and her father's chin. She wasn't particularly keen to be an actress, and today farms in the country. One day she invited several of us to an unforgettable party at the Hulberts' home in Curzon Street. Jack and Cis, then at their zenith, were kindness itself. They made us feel at home at once, and the knowledge that we were actually to spend an evening with two of the greatest stars of our time was an excitement in itself. One of their guests was a famous and good-looking agent named Ivor McLaren. He asked me what I wanted to be in the theatre, and roared with laughter when I told him that I never expected to get further than playing maids' parts in the West End. Since maids are now non-existent in plays, it is lucky for me that things turned out differently. He asked me to go and see him when I had finished school. I did, but by then I had married Michael and was already under way as an actress.

Michael spent only a year at the school, having been seen at one end-of-term performance by Michael MacOwan, and offered a job at the Westminster Theatre where J. B. Priestley and Ronald Jeans were running a repertory season of first-class plays, and paying tiny salaries in the hope of breaking 'even. It was a magnificent training ground, though the money was only £3 a week, less half a crown insurance. Hitler put paid to the venture. The first season in 1938 kept going through the Munich crisis and until the following spring; and the second struggled valiantly through the first few months of the war. An aunt of mine who, until Chamberlain returned with 'Peace in our time', had generously offered to take me with her daughters to the comparative safety of Wales, precipitated my engagement to Michael. He didn't like the thought of being without me, and proposed by letter. I accepted, and my last two terms were even better than the others had been, every day having the kind of magic that being young and in love and at the start of one's life's work can give.

In my fifth term I was offered a job myself, and to my shock and horror was told that 'J.D.' had turned it down out of hand. In view of my financial situation this was a monstrous thing to do, and I was extremely angry. Michael was an enormous help to me throughout that period. He had been a great favourite with the staff as well as with the students, who were certain that he had above average talent, and were furious about our engagement since they felt that marriage at such an early age might handicap his career. Neither of us cared what they thought, believing it to be entirely our own affair. My days were full, and Michael, since he was understudying during the day as well as acting at night, was even busier, but we found ways of being together.

That fifth term I played Bunty in *The Vortex*, written by Noël Coward and directed by Alison Leggatt, and suddenly I began to realize what acting was all about for me. I was once told by a man who had been in Special Branch that the word for someone who had been politically brainwashed, and in whom the brainwashing had 'taken', was the 'click'. I had the 'click' in *The Vortex*. It was a small but definite revelation.

My sixth and final term arrived, and since the state of Michael's and my finances was even worse than usual, and we were longing to get married, it was imperative that I had some good parts to show to important people like agents, who would be coming to the end-of-term shows. To my horror, the best part I was given was the seventy-year-old landlady in *At Mrs Beam's*. It was certainly a good role, but of a kind that I was unlikely to be called upon to play for the next half century. I was outraged. The school had already done the dirty on me by turning down a job on my behalf; now they were prejudicing my chances again. With Michael at my elbow, I complained forcefully, and was eventually given Laura in *Still Life* (now better known as *Brief Encounter*) and Celia in *As You Like It*. I still had one character part, though, but I solved my difficulties by wearing a very beautiful white wig, and putting on the best make-up I knew how. Funnily enough, it was this play which netted me no less than three offers. One was for repertory in Hunstanton, twice nightly, twice weekly. This would have meant eight parts a month, and forty-eight performances! I wanted to do it very much, but Michael was worried that after two years mostly on a starvation diet, I wouldn't be able to stand it. In the event I had an almost unbelievable stroke of luck, which also came about through that one performance.

A. R. Whatmore, then a leading London director, a well-known comedy actor, and a playwright, had been approached by the Donald brothers who ran Her Majesty's Theatre in Aberdeen, to head and direct a repertory company there. Rodney Millington, who had just started the famous casting directory, *Spotlight*, was engaged to do the casting. He engaged Stewart Granger and his first wife, Elspeth March, as the leads, and having seen Michael at the Westminster, immediately wrote to him offering him the male juvenile leads. Michael's contract still had three months to run, so he couldn't accept, and after it was over Terence Rattigan had asked him to play a small part in his new play, *After the Dance*, to be produced in London in the summer. However, the salary that Millington was offering was £8 10s. a week—riches to us. Michael decided not to send his refusal by letter, but to call on Rodney Millington and explain. He told him how much he would have liked to accept, because he wanted to get married. 'Is your fiancée an actress?' asked Millington. 'She's leaving the Webber-Douglas at the end of this term.' 'What's her name?' When Michael told him, Rodney frowned and began rummaging through some papers. He found a Webber-Douglas programme, and flourished it under Michael's nose. 'I knew it! I knew it!' he exclaimed. 'Look!' He had put three asterisks beside my name, which was his highest personal rating. 'Why not have her in the company too?' And then and there he offered £6 10s. Fifteen pounds a week between us! What a chance! We couldn't afford to miss it.

Michael MacOwan was sympathetic. Ronald Jeans gave us his blessing, but Mr Priestley was on holiday somewhere and couldn't be found. The suspense of the next few days was agonizing, but at last he was run to earth in Stratford-on-Avon. He too allowed us to accept the offer, but with one proviso: that Michael should rejoin his company the following season. Throughout our professional lives, Jack Priestley has been the best and kindest of friends. When Michael came out of the army in 1946, he offered him a job as soon as he heard he had been demobbed.

Dulcie Gray is not my real name. I was christened Dulcie Bailey. There is a ruling in Equity which forbids two actors or actresses to have the same name. Someone already had mine, and just at the time I was preparing to go on the stage, she was playing the maid in *The French for Love* at the Criterion. Gray was my mother's maiden name, so it was an easy choice, though for a while I toyed with more exotic names such as Dawn Forrest, and Pearl Sunshine. I even for a brief time decided on Angela Botibol, on the grounds that the name would be memorable, even if my performances were not.

Five days after my training was over, Michael and I got married. He was exhausted from a long and arduous engagement (in the theatre!), but managed to get us a special licence to be married in church. I bought a blue suit for my wedding dress, a hat, shoes, handbag and going-away dress, all for less than £8. My going-away dress, in fact, cost fifteen shillings! My mother, who was on leave, refused her consent although she liked Michael very much, on the grounds that a few weeks of settled work and a bank balance of twenty-seven pounds was too precarious a basis for marriage. Fortunately she relented and came to the wedding. I've always been glad about that. It was to be the last time we saw her. Less than three years later she was killed by the Japanese as she tried to escape from Malaya by ship. On the way back from the vestry Michael whispered fondly, 'One minute on the way to our Golden Wedding.' I have seldom felt more tired.

The war came. The age of innocence was over. I'm glad I didn't choose Pearl Sunshine as a name, and gladder still that I went to the Webber-Douglas.

Patrick Macnee

Patrick Macnee was born in London in 1922 and educated at Summer-
fields and Eton. He spent 9 months at the Webber-Douglas School in
1940, then joined a repertory company in Letchworth Garden City.
After a spell in rep at Prince's Theatre, Bradford, he toured as Laurie
in Little Women, *which played at the Westminster Theatre, London*
for 3 months. In October 1942 he was called up and served in the
RNVR, commanding a motor torpedo boat.

After the war he worked with Peter Glenville at the Lyric, Hammer-
smith, and then played in The White Devil *with Margaret Rawlings*
and Robert Helpman at the Duchess Theatre in 1947. After the birth
of his son Rupert, he says, he did 'anything to earn money' : he was an
extra in Olivier's Hamlet, *worked with David Niven in* The Elusive
Pimpernel *('largely because I could ride horses'), and in fact made a*
number of films before going into rep at Windsor for a year in 1951. In
1952 he did revivals of various plays in London, and finally left for
Canada. He now makes his home in Palm Springs, California.

In 1972–3 he played in Sleuth *for sixteen months in New York,*
and in 1976 was Dr Watson to Roger Moore's Sherlock Holmes in a
Hollywood television show. He is perhaps best known for the immensely
popular television series, The Avengers.

I'm proud, enormously proud. I've been an actor for thirty-seven years and I have played in all sorts of parts. I am proud of my versatility, of my craft. For that is what acting is—a craft. One different from that of a dentist or a skilled fireman, but a craft just the same. It is this craft which allowed me, last Sunday, to fly to Johannesburg to make a commercial for the new Rover, that will next week help me when I visit Edmonton to compere one of their spectacular shows, *The Eleventh Commonwealth Games Gala*, which will feature others with different crafts, from Olivia Newton John to Cleo Laine.

Why do I exercise my craft in this way? For money, yes; but also because money made from making, say, commercials, allows me to undertake roles for which I am less well paid. For instance, this summer I hope to play with Diana Rigg at Chichester and then I trust I shall be using my craft for ends more rewarding than those that are simply financial.

Can the acting craft be entirely learnt, can drama schools prepare a man for a hurly-burly profession that may require him to advertise a Rover car one week and play in a Shakespeare tragedy the next? Are actors born rather than made?

They tell me I was born in London on February 6th, 1922. There were no actors or actresses in my family. True, my great grandfather, Sir Daniel Macnee, had been a famous portrait painter who painted women most beautifully. Otherwise, my background was one of hunting, shooting, fishing and horse-racing. My father, in fact, was a racehorse trainer. So there were no artistic or theatrical influences at home.

It was at my preparatory school, Summerfields, that I first became interested in drama. There I played all the major parts in Shakespeare before I was eleven. Then I went to Eton and performed in all these roles again. Now, when I look back, I think I learnt more about acting at Eton than at my 'official' drama school which I was to enter when I was 17. Many people have misconceptions about Eton. They do not think of it, for instance, as a highly-developed artistic centre. Yet it is, and many of the pupils there go on to become eminent in the arts. (Among my own contemporaries were Michael Bentine, Humphrey Lyttelton, Dennis Cannon, William Douglas Home and, not least, Ludovic Kennedy, who played drums in the school orchestra and was dazzlingly charismatic.)

But let me be frank. At Eton I never felt I had a personality of my own. I never felt at home and never developed lasting friendships. Perhaps that is why I became an actor. For actors are often shy people, quite lonely people (an only son or an only daughter), and not at all extroverted as so many understandably believe. They hide their shyness behind a theatrical façade and the better they act the more others are fooled. As a schoolboy, I was already daydreaming that one day I would be a famous actor. I dreamed I was dashing Leslie Howard in *The Scarlet Pimpernel* or suave Rex Harrison in *French Without Tears*. Meanwhile, under the auspices of Sir Robin Darwin who ran the so-called Drawing Schools at Eton I performed in an ambitious programme of plays. As a 16-year old, I even played old Queen Victoria in *Victoria Regina*! Michael Benthall directed many of these plays and I learnt much from him.

I had no other idea than of going on the stage. I had no other thought—in terms of a future profession—than going to a drama school. One of my friends at Eton was Derrick Beecham, a nephew of Sir Thomas. (It was always Derrick's job to change the great man's drenched shirt collars in the intervals, when Sir Thomas came to Eton to conduct at the school concerts.) Derrick Beecham told me that he had a relation studying at the Webber-Douglas Drama School. 'It's better than RADA,' he said. I had my sights on RADA so this pronouncement was disturbing. Webber-Douglas had the advantage, I was persuaded to believe, of being smaller than RADA and less 'establishment'. Perhaps I was persuaded wrongly. Sometimes I wish I had gone to RADA for it might have been a place more exciting for me, better for me.

Anyway, I chose Webber-Douglas that crisis-torn summer of 1939. Not long after hearing Neville Chamberlain pronounce 'We are now at war' on the wireless I went along to Webber-Douglas for my audition in the Chanticleer, the school's small theatre. The buildings were housed in two connecting early Victorian villas in Clareville Street, South Kensington. The theatre had been added. For my audition I had chosen a speech from *King Henry V*:

'Upon the king!—let us our lives, our souls,
Our debts, our careful wives, our children, and
Our sins lay on the king! We must bear all ...'

And this I declaimed in front of the ex-opera singer Johnstone Douglas, the effective director of the school, an immensely polite, tentative man with a beautiful speaking voice, who, apart from the fencing master, was the only male on the staff. Two others also listened to me—one of whom was the Irish actress Ellen O'Malley who had once played in the first productions of several Shaw plays. She was already an old lady.

I was a 17-year-old youth with acne, and innocent of women, and given to blushing. But my audition must have gone well because they awarded me a scholarship. No doubt, too, they were anxious for men to attend the school for they guessed, rightly, that the war would considerably reduce the number of their male students. I was to begin the next term, in January, 1940.

January, 1940. The time of the 'Phoney war', the songs like 'We'll Hang Out the Washing on the Siegfried Line', the air raid shelters with sandbags, and there I was, a spotty adolescent aware that soon enough the war would claim me, that my days at drama school were to be but a brief interlude. In fact, it was ludicrous going to drama school then. Because of the shortage of male students it was hard to take the training seriously. The preponderance of women made the Webber-Douglas seem more like a finishing school for young ladies than a place to learn one's life craft.

Still, a 17-year-old youth, even one self-conscious with spots, should have rejoiced at such an array of girls, girls, girls— Mamie the blonde milkmaid, two gorgeous dark Pamelas, a sophisticated Celia always dressed in black and wearing pearls like a vamp-spy, Sheila from Aberdeen with red-golden hair and grey eyes; these and shapely others dressed in black leotards for the ballet and mime classes left me in a state of breathless shock as I watched them moving gracefully. So many gloriously-shaped bottoms moving in front of me. How I stared! You see, I was totally naïve and inexperienced in the heterosexual sense. From all those boys at Eton to all these girls at Webber-Douglas—what a change in the climate! You cannot be at boarding school from the age of 8 to 17 without having some sexual encounters with members of your own sex, though there are those who do not care to admit such things. The fact is a public schoolboy has to *graduate* to heterosexuality. That's but one thing I am grateful to the Webber-Douglas school for. I was moving in that joyful direction which would take me to graduation day. Not that one did anything serious at the school, really. I remember there was one exciting young lady whom I used to go home with. What I did there was to help her comb her hair.

There were other pertinent extra-curricular activities. Oh, the pleasures and advantages of a drama-student even in wartime. With other Webber-Douglas students I shared lodgings. In that house, too, was a RADA student, Ian Carmichael, who became a good friend. All of us spent most of our money in going to plays and films in the West End. I learnt as much from watching actors I admired as at school. Laurence Olivier, for instance, in *Macbeth;* John Gielgud in *The Importance of Being Ernest;* Alec Guinness in his modern dress *Hamlet.*

Of course I learnt something at the Webber-Douglas. I felt affectionately towards one of the drama teachers, Ellen O'Malley, for she was gentle, encouraging and full of humour. She was always losing her spectacles or her pencils and diving into a vast bag she carried around. She liked me, too—maybe because I was half Irish. Under her direction I played Orlando to an assortment of Rosalinds. The surplus of girls meant each one could play only one act. A very fat girl, Bridget Lansbury, played Audrey—later she changed her name to Angela and became very well known as a comedy actress. Sheila Burrell and Sheila Keith were two other actresses who were later to become known and who were my contemporaries.

At Webber-Douglas we were supposed to be taught how to sing, how to act, how to breathe, etc. Most of these things I learnt after I left drama school but the main thing I learnt there was the ability to direct, something which I have done in California. It is one of my unknown talents which nobody remotely cares about, but at Webber-Douglas I was allowed to take control of a group of people and direct them in aspects of the theatre. And there were some remarkable actors at the school. The best was Geoffrey Hibbert, now dead. His first film was *Love on the Dole* (also Deborah Kerr's first film). He was a genius of a young actor.

I stayed only nine months at the Webber-Douglas. If nothing else it was an introduction to a theatrical atmosphere. But those months were unreal. The war was the reality. During the day classes in mime, ballet, modern dancing, voice production, verse speaking, someone continually calling out 'Push out your diaphragm.' During the night the walks back to South Kensington from a West-End theatre through blacked-out streets while an air-raid warning sounded grimly and searchlights probed the skies.

That summer I remember hearing the news about Dunkirk. I was strolling up Clareville Grove. There was a marvellous scent of lilac everywhere. Nowadays I can't smell lilac without recalling those disturbing days of the war, that time and that place. In August, a fire-bomb landed on the school, so war came directly to the Webber-Douglas. For me, too, it was the end of an episode. I read an advertisement in *The Stage* and went to join a Repertory Company in Letchworth Garden City. I was still learning my craft, but a year later the real savage world of war caught up with me and I was in the Navy.

Yvonne Mitchell

Yvonne Mitchell was born in London. She was trained at the London Theatre Studio, and worked in rep at Birmingham, Oxford and Bristol. She spent a season at the Old Vic (including Ophelia) in 1950, and a season at Stratford (including The Taming of the Shrew) *in 1952. She won awards for her film roles in* Woman in a Dressing-Gown *and* The Divided Heart. *Her television appearances include* Cheri *(1973).*

Miss Mitchell is a well-known author whose writings include the award-winning play, The Same Sky, *eight novels (the most recent being* But Answer Came There None, *1977), three children's books, and a biography of Colette.*

In the late 'thirties one left school at O-level age, fifteen or sixteen, without any idea not only of what one wanted to do, but of what there was to do. I knew nothing whatsoever of the theatre; I had been taken by my father to see The Crazy Gang at the Victoria Palace, and by my grandmother each Christmas to a pantomime. At school, though I was unable to keep in tune, the only experience I had had of acting was singing the Second Page in *As You Like It*. So I decided on a theatre career.

How I managed to meet a teacher from RADA I don't remember. I was fat, and wearing a thick pink and white woolly coat which didn't help. 'My advice,' he said, 'is that you might succeed in spite of RADA, but certainly not because of it. Why don't you try for an audition with Michel St Denis?'

I learnt some lines of Desdemona and went to the Queen's Theatre in Shaftesbury Avenue. Perhaps I was wearing my pink fattening coat, certainly my hair would have been unbrushed, and my stockings 'down-gyvèd' to the ankles. In those days I despised looking presentable, possibly because my step-mother was always beautifully dressed. In the dark auditorium were Michel St Denis and George Devine. I did my piece at top speed, and they asked me to come down and talk to them.

'Why,' asked Michel, with his fascinating French accent,

'did you say it all in a far corner and wiz your back to us?'

I didn't know I had. Without answering his question I said, 'Could you tell me please if I'm in or not?'

'Alright. Yes,' he replied, and George Devine nodded.

I can't think what they saw in me, and I believe neither could they; because when the LTS (the London Theatre Studio) closed down not long afterwards because the war started, Michel's final advice to me was 'Why don't you get married?'

My father was convinced that anything to do with the theatre must be immoral. He always, literally, fell off his seat laughing at the Crazy Gang and clambered back saying harshly each time: 'I hope you didn't understand that.' But he agreed to pay the fees 'on condition', as he told Michel, 'that she never plays a loose woman.'

I didn't, during my training, ever play a 'loose woman', but I played a number of things my father understood less, because a great deal of our training was based on our own invention. I invented, for instance, an old crone whose hanging breasts beneath her jumper were two (mimed) unstoppered gin bottles, at which she would take swigs now and then by throwing them up towards her mouth. I invented a penguin, and a rocking open-mouthed idiot for a dance based on Goya's war pictures. Most of the creatures the students chose to invent were old, ugly and vulgar; our imagination not being fertile, and our desire to get away from our own immature, fat, thin, knock-kneed or otherwise self-conscious selves being uppermost in our desires.

We were not encouraged to get away from our ugliness, only from our self-consciousness. To that end, Motley had designed for us, boys and girls alike, very short grey sleeveless tunics which just covered our grey schoolgirl-type knickers, so that our worst features were daily exposed. We wore these tunics for everything; for acrobatics, voice lessons, mime, improvisation and dance; therefore our inventions had to be from the imagination, and convincing without the aid of outward appearance. For the plays which we rehearsed (a Greek drama, a musical play based on the bible Judith, a restoration comedy, a Tchekov, a Shakespeare), we had additionally two beautifully-cut circular pieces of grey cloth, one of which we used as a skirt and the other as a cloak; and it was in these garments that we went out to lunch at a café in Upper Street, by Islington Green, near the passage down which was housed the LTS in what had once been a chapel.

My drama school did nothing to prepare us for the theatre of our day, nor for the decade after the war, though all our teaching would have been relevant to the theatre of today. In those days what we did was considered eccentric, even 'phoney', and indeed very few of us ever, after our training, could fit into the Shaftesbury Avenue world.

The most brilliant student was Merula Salaman, who later married Alec Guinness. She was, as far as I know, never employed in the commercial theatre, but her gifts would have been invaluable today. Imaginative, strange, she was able to create reality with no help from words, costume or staging, simply by her belief. I remember her now—no, I don't remember *her* at all—I remember the goat she turned into, which I really believed hoofed its four-footed way up a stone spiral such as one sees at the zoo (the platform she was *actually* on was flat and wooden), and having frightened itself when it got to the top, began calling urgently for its mate, whilst chewing a branch of oak-leaves, before hoof-sliding down again. How *did* I, *do* I, believe they were oakleaves? That was her secret, her power of belief, conveyable in every imaginative detail to her audience. Of course there was no place for her in drawing-room comedy.

I remember a group of students in a Cornish village by the sea. My memory as spectator tells me it was Cornish or Breton, though it was of course on that same flat daïs as Merula's goat-crag. The women hung out their washing—no clothes, no clothes-line—and called to each other in no known language, the chat of women neighbours the world over, calling above the cry of the seagulls (the cries made ventriloquist-fashion by the women themselves), the wind and the pounding of the sea.

I remember a student climbing up a non-existent rope-ladder to a frighteningly high trapeze, and swinging as circus trapezists do across a vast area of sand and soil far below, clinging on to the perilous bar with her hands, and then turning in mid-air so that she hung by her feet. That is the impression that remains with me of a prim little fair-haired girl called Bay White, in a grey tunic on a flat stage.

We were taught how to develop our powers of belief and observation so that we could mime our intentions with conviction, but we were never taught who or what to be, or how to accomplish any feat. We were taught to notice what happened to the muscles of our legs as we climbed or descended stairs, so that the movement could eventually be accomplished without the actual stairs being there. We were taught to notice what shape our hands took as they picked up an object, so that that object could eventually be dispensed with, and our audience see it because its shape was there. We were sent to the zoo to study any animal we chose, and understand its movement and its motive for moving, until we had absorbed its identity. I shall never now lose my love of penguins, having, I believe, once been one.

These Mime classes, as they were called, were not so much 'taught' as watched, by Michel. He was cruel in criticism but never attempted to teach by bullying. He had enormous strength, physical, moral and mental, but would not admit weakness in others. He never talked to us professorially—there were in any case lectures on the Greek theatre and Japanese Noh plays by professors—but always in the physical language an actor can understand; with sometimes a lack of good English which made his meaning even more expressive. His great strength as a teacher lay in his vivid imagination and his power to communicate it. He could make his pupils act being cold by a description of the weather which would freeze them. He called our weak efforts 'pi-pi', but would also be delighted by any sign of truth. 'Ah!' he muttered as he watched a student—

not long afterwards killed in the war—performing an old and dirty man who walked with stiff difficulty, 'Ah, yes! He has a private disease of his own.' He was patient with beginners, impatient of excuses, and expected of us near-impossible powers of endurance. In a Greek play where two pupils were to represent a fountain, he made one unfortunate girl stand motionless with the other on her back for hour-long rehearsals. In vain did the standing girl protest, weep, and even get a certificate from her doctor; Michel ignored it, carried on with rehearsals and eventual performance, and at the end of the term asked her to leave. Had she ever gone on the stage this would have been invaluable training for the endurance expected of actors by directors the world over.

Our Improvisation classes were taken by George Devine. Their development, like those of the mime classes, could take a whole term. Of course, you cannot become a penguin or a goat overnight. But improvisation aimed, not at an animal, nor at accomplishing a feat, but at a character, and eventually at an improvised play. At the beginning of the term about sixteen of us were left in a small room, each to invent and become someone. Whether we were to start from a thought, from an observation, or from a physical characteristic didn't matter; different actors grow in different ways. Most of us sat around the room on the floor for that first hour wondering how on earth to start; none of us dared to get up and move. By the second or third 'class' we had realized that none of the others was the least bit interested in what we would do, so absorbed were they either in their own inadequacies or their own thoughts; so our concentration grew deeper, we could blot out the others, forget them, and live each in his own world, despite the cramped space. Only one girl remained rigidly cynical and did nothing but smirk at the others' grotesque beginnings, but the training itself taught us to ignore such deliberate intrusions. I can in fact even now concentrate on what I am doing, reading, or thinking, when there are other people talking or watching the television around me. I learnt this absorption particularly in these classes, so that years later in an open-air production, I was not worried by dogs barking, birds, or a young man in the audience repeating the lines as we spoke them, in a very loud voice, to his deaf grandmother.

These Improvisation classes, which eventually became plays, were in the vein of the work Michel had done with his own 'Compagnie des Quinze' in France. That company had a writer and a designer as part of their group. I believe, however, that their work differed from ours—apart from being professional and extremely accomplished—because the writer, André Obey, had an idea, the actors worked on it, and the writer then, from their improvisation, wrote it. This method is as old as Goldoni, and employed today by such companies as Joint Stock. A fine example of the work of the 'Compagnie des Quinze' is a play in which the idea, or basis, is the river Loire and its tributaries. Eight of the actresses went to the district and apportioned themselves a tributary each, to study. The result was a play, *Mother Loire*, about a large, dominant, sweeping woman and her seven daughters, some weak, some unreliable, all seemingly independent, and yet relying totally on their mother for their existence.

We students had no resident playwright, and no one started us off with an idea, yet we aimed at making a whole play. What George Devine told us to do was to 'become' any character we liked, provided that that character was our own invention.

It was perhaps during the second or third hour of an improvisation class that some of us got up and tested our movements. The first intimation I got of the dirty old gin-swigger I was to become, was a habit or tic I developed, whilst still sitting, of clicking my tongue whilst throwing my eyes up to heaven, as if to express disapprobation of something my old self had seen or heard. Of course we all developed, however varied our characters, into the lame, the peculiar, the dirty, the mad, because our immature imaginations would take years before they could grasp the young, the simple, the beautiful or the clean.

After leaving us alone for perhaps five or six of these classes, George then told us to look around at each other and wonder if any of the creatures we had become could find themselves in the same place, society, or situation as any of the others. One aged couple decided they were married and set about devising a weekend at the seaside, where they sat up all night in a double bed playing cards and grunting as they cheated each other. At this stage we were allowed to 'dress up' and I remember Tommy Heathcote's clay pipe, and Sonia South's mass of woolly scarves which she kept on in bed. Sonia later married a 'bargee' as they were then called, and brought up her three children on the canals, and became responsible for the government's eventually agreeing to allow bargees' children an education at the different schools on their route.

Merula improvised a fat-bottomed old lavatory attendant, continually wiping seats in a circular motion, with a filthy old cloth, and flushing the cistern. Those characters who joined her decided that the 'ladies' was at Lords' Cricket Ground, which suited John Earle who had become a dreadful old blimp, and now found a situation for himself by getting into the 'ladies' by mistake. The playlet which had started off funnily enough then developed into total consternation and finally chaos. My old gin-swigger found a number of characters to board with in the Old Kent Road, including a formidably bossy landlady and one particularly frail old lady (Lalage Lewis with a coat-hanger for an ear-trumpet), who choked to death on a fish bone in the middle of a meal, which led, as the other playlet had done, to consternation and chaos.

Our other classes were less wild. We started each morning with acrobatics, taken by a gym instructor whom I feared. I particularly disliked doing 'lions' leaps', which meant leaping over the bent backs of two other students into a somersault. A few of the boys achieved it eventually, perhaps even one or two of the girls, but I gained nothing from my attempts but a slipped sacro-iliac which has incapacitated me from time to time ever since.

Voice lessons were traditional; a-a-a-ah, letting out the breath slowly, reciting 'Mumbo-jumbo-god-of-the-Congo-mumbo-jumbo-will-hoo-doo-you-' etc, until one ran out of breath; and singing lessons from which Mary Alexander and I were turned out because we sang flat, and for which I was grateful as I objected to putting my hand on the fat old man's stomach as he demonstrated how to breathe.

But the relaxation lessons were invaluable. We lay on our backs on the floor, as near sleep as we could, and then learnt—keeping all the other muscles relaxed—to tense one: in a forearm, then, relaxing that, in a calf, an eyelid and so on. Eventually we could recite a long Shakespeare speech holding a heavy table above our heads, our arm muscles tensed, but our throat and neck muscles free.

The dance lessons, taken by Suria Magito, who some time later married Michel, were built once more on characters, based on Goya or Breughel paintings or bible stories, taken to performance standard with specially written music and specially designed costumes.

One of our directors of plays was Marius Goring. Our chief fear of his rehearsals lay in the fact that he considered nothing physically impossible, and dealt as ruthlessly with physical fear as did our acrobatics teacher, and as Michel dealt with lack of endurance. In directing *A Midsummer Night's Dream* Marius had a fairy guarding the sleeping Titania pushed off a high rostrum, and insisted she did it backwards without bending her knees. As the feat was impossible except by an experienced stuntman, the sixteen-year-old student, who was in any case gently unco-ordinated, could but attempt it each time, fail, fall with bent knees, and be sent back up the rostrum to try again. Marius was already a known professional actor in the commercial theatre, as was George Devine, though I believe neither had had experience of directing before and were learning how to by dealing with our inadequacies.

But apart from Michel there were other highly professional and brilliant people around us. The Motleys (as Margaret and Sophie Harris and Elizabeth Montgomery called themselves) were perhaps the best designers in London, and whilst designing for the Old Vic and the London theatres still found time to create and make our costumes for the end of term plays. Suria Magito was a well-known dancer and choreographer, Professor Isaacs was the greatest living authority on the Greek theatre, and once or twice a term the magical greatest actor in England, John Gielgud, would take a Shakespeare class. Though we were not worthy of them we unmistakably knew their worth. There was also Bert who taught us make-up in a painterly fashion, showing us that light colours brought forward a feature, and dark colours sunk it. Those students with prominent nose bones put dark brown down the length; I used it for my nose tip because it was too long, and for my jaws because they were too wide. Marriott Longman turned, with the knowledge of how to emphasize certain features and withdraw others, in one half-hour from a pale, long-faced English girl whose very demeanour showed that she thought she was ugly, into a confident and volatile Spanish beauty.

Most of the students, unlike Merula, were no more adept at any of the classes than I was. Although there was some talent, most of it was spasmodic, unsustained. There was Gene Jessel, a passionately emotional girl, who was so soon to be drowned together with a whole shipful of children being evacuated to America, whose talent lacked communication; there was Mary Alexander who could conjure Titania magically with her voice but was less at ease with her body. These two were from rigidly Roman Catholic backgrounds, whose parents, I believe, were as worried as my father about the immorality of the theatre. There was a Chinese girl whom we called Jin, a Singhalese boy called Dudley Misso, whose pulsing epiglottis and liquid eyes as he sat motionless, miming a toad, I shall not forget. He lived through the bombing of London though he was buried for twenty-four hours under rubble, his fingers linked with his girl-friend's, and later became leader of a night-club dance band. There was beautiful Angelica Bell, daughter of Vanessa Bell and Duncan Grant, whose talents turned to painting and who never played on a stage. There was Peter Ustinov, who could imitate Michel so brilliantly that we believed he was in the room, and whose 'doctor' with a waiting-room full of patients was an hilarious half-hour. There was Chattie, Merula's sister, beautiful as a ginger kitten, who now runs Common Stock, which works with and plays to schools. There was James Donald, James Cairncross and Noel Willman, who did manage in spite of their training to get into the theatre as it then was. As for myself, as can be judged by Michel's farewell advice to me, I was a poor student, but I had one gift: that of listening; though it was not until years later that I understood what I had heard and began to put it into effect. It was, for instance, years before I actually understood that breathing is the basic necessity for becoming someone else; for turning the word or the thought into flesh. As a man breathes, so he is; as a man breathes such is his mood; as a man breathes, such is his rhythm of life. And as an actor has to *learn* to breathe someone else's life, it must, every time he plays a part, become less a knowledge that he is breathing in that man's rhythm, and more an instinct.

Our end of term show marked our progress for us and for our teachers, but our parents were dismayed. It seemed to bear no resemblance to what they expected us to be learning. Why should we display ourselves as inmates of an asylum? Or sing our Greek or biblical choruses in this weird twelve-toned scale? Their dismay, even disappointment, was understandable, though my father took his incomprehension a little further when I attempted to play a young girl in a scene from

Farquhar's *The Beaux' Stratagem*. His only comment to me on my performance, which I admit was a feeble one, was: 'Why you should use a door that nobody else used I shall never know.'

Though our stage was small and the auditorium even smaller —four rows of wooden seats—I found difficulty in being heard past the first one. My natural voice disappeared to a deadened whisper when I attempted to 'feel' an emotion, and when I raised my voice the emotion disappeared in a spate of words without meaning. I opted for the first method, it being less painful to myself, and let the audience suffer what it might, keeping my 'mumbo-jumbo-god-of-the-Congo' breathing technique for voice classes without applying what I had learnt there to an actual play; though of course I mmmm-ed, aaaa-ed and hmm-ed daily—at a bus stop, in the bath, in a train— for years after I had left the studio. Eccentricities, and indifference to the fact that someone might be looking or listening were, I suppose, part of the training. And though we were expected to attempt everything, to succeed was not in the curriculum; though when a genuine spark appeared in a student, however transitory, Michel was as delighted as if a dog had spoken.

Each of us remembers those student days quite differently. Chattie thinks they made us arrogant: 'I was convinced at the time,' she said, 'that we students were better than any others, but looking back I realize how appallingly bad we were.' Peter Ustinov thought the training arty. Some of the students remember it as too cruel; destructive of self-confidence. I believe it was, but I don't believe that self-confidence is what a young actor should have, so I was content with it, more than content: I adored it.

It had in any case taken me away from my bourgeois background into a world of magical possibility, and among friends, young girls and boys like myself who were ill-at-ease in their own family background, and found here for the first time the realization that they were not odd, nor outcasts, but simply belonged to a different world from the one in which they had been brought up.

Mai Zetterling

Mai Zetterling graduated from the National Theatre School in Stockholm in 1943. After becoming a very successful actress at the National Theatre, and making such films with Ingmar Bergman as Frenzy *and* Music in the Dark, *she came to London in 1947 to make her first film for Ealing Studios,* Frieda. *Other British films include* Quartet, Hildegard, The Main Attraction, Only Two Can Play, *etc. Her West End stage appearances began with* The Wild Duck *in 1948, and include* The Doll's House, The Creditors, Point of Departure, Restless Heart, The Seagull, *etc.*

In 1963 her short feature film, The War Game, *won first prize at Venice. She has co-written and directed several documentaries for the BBC, including the award-winning* Vincent the Dutchman. *She is the author of a children's book* (The Cat's Tale), *two novels* (Night Games, Bird of Passage), *and a book of short stories* (Shadow of the Sun). *Swedish films she has co-written and directed number* Loving Couples, Night Games, Dr Glas *and* The Girls. *Other films she has co-written and directed include* Visions of Eight *(on the Munich Olympics);* The Moon is a Green Cheese, *a film for children; and a film on Stockholm for Canadian television. At present she is engaged on a documentary film for the BBC about Greenland.*

'She is pigeon-toed, lisps, and is inclined to baby talk, but she has talent.' An aunt of mine—certainly not my favourite one—sent the press cutting to me. I was fifteen at the time, the country Sweden, the city Stockholm, the play written by the Nobel prize-winner Per Lagerkvist. I came to be playing the lead in it having overheard a chance remark in a tram that a young girl was wanted for a part in this production. I had by then given up the idea of becoming a sailor or an explorer—my first and second choices of profession—since in neither was there a tradition for women, I was told, and had instead settled to become an actress. I don't really know why— I was teased mercilessly by everyone in my working-class family, who had jobs as factory workers, bicycle repairers, shop assistants. My father was a top-hat maker. No wonder they all laughed; it was an outlandish idea, it was the wrong world for someone like me. So in the end I had shut up, finished school when I was just fourteen, and had started out on the same road as my family, packing parcels and running errands, until that day in an overcrowded tram.

I was one of fifteen girls auditioning for the part, and it was the first time I had ever been in a theatre, yet strangely enough I was not scared. Somehow I took it for granted that I would get the part.

The review my aunt sent me was for my own good, as she

put it; success could make me big-headed. She really needn't have worried about that, as my opinion of myself was very low indeed. I was a mouse of a girl, neither pretty nor ugly, too small for my age, so full of social inferiority that I never spoke until spoken to, and kept my eyes firmly on the ground.

At the time of this extraordinary piece of luck I was working in a factory, my job being to take the tacking out of men's overcoats. The only relief from the monotony of it all was going Friday and Saturday nights to some packed and seedy dance-palace or other. I started to believe it might be possible to become an actress although everybody warned me not to take this chance too seriously. 'It is very difficult, my dear, to become an actress, and it's a very insecure life'—my mother, of course, had all the built-in prejudices about the theatrical world, with its corruption, drinking, parties, sex; no, I must learn some kind of job that would give me security and stability. What? Well, a shop assistant, my family thought, so I went to school for half a year to try to learn to be one, but wrote poems on the textbooks that told me that a customer was always right.

I rebelled, and signed a strange contract for a summer tour in the provinces. We were to visit children's holiday camps on bicycles. The contract said we would be provided with food and lodging, but no money, not even pocket money. Sometimes the lodgings turned out to be a haystack or a boat-house, the meals might be porridge or just bread and water, but I came back to Stockholm happy, lean and dirty, and decided that was the life for me. In the meantime I had to earn some money so I took a job at a pawnbrokers, where I dusted vases and scrubbed out old cupboards, while in the early evening I swept the floors of a small children's theatre, where I also managed to get a part as a witch.

That's how I met Calle. 'A man who knows the subject thoroughly, a man so soaked in it that he eats it, sleeps it, and dreams it, a man who always teaches with success, no matter how little he knows of technical pedagogy.' I was lucky enough to meet such a man, an eccentric with a possibly even more

eccentric mother. Such people are rare in the city of Stockholm, but there they were, the two of them, larger than life.
I consider my meeting with Calle one of the most important of
my life; he was a kind of guru, impossible, demanding, selfish,
but also enthusiastic, totally giving, loving, and he certainly
stood out in a crowd of impeccable Swedes. 'My dear girl,' he
said in the dressing-room after the performance, 'you've got
talent, you must learn something about acting. Come to my
school and I'll teach you.'

But how could I? There was no money for such things—I
earned barely enough to exist. His reply was, 'Come to my
school three evenings a week. Tuition will be free.' There I
played everything from *Mädchen in Uniform*, operettas by
Lehar, silly nonsenses like *The White Horse Inn* and *No, No,
Nanette*, but also Strindberg, Shakespeare and Lorca. I sang, I
danced, I cried, I laughed, for a whole year under his guidance.
And how I grew!

It's difficult to be precise about Calle's quality as a teacher.
He used to say, 'I want to *un-teach*', and that is perhaps the best
way to describe his method. He suggested things rather than
saying how they should be done. When he mimed a scene for
us—with great vigour and in a way that could only be called
ham-acting, he would always say afterwards, 'But you do it
your own way, of course.' The less inventive among us would
try to imitate him, which was not altogether good for them.
Calle certainly did not like it; he would get angry and hot and
as red as the fez he wore, and tell them to do the scene over
again but in a different way. For instance, if it was a dramatic
scene he would demand that they turn it into a farce, or he
would change the roles around so that sometimes Ophelia
would play Hamlet, and Hamlet Ophelia, to the great amuse-
ment of all of us watching. But it was more than just fun
because afterwards, dissecting it with Calle, we could clearly
see the pitfalls for an actor in that particular scene, as well as
the possible sources of irony. Together we learnt new ways of
coming to grips with the scene. He was a great admirer of

Stanislavski, so we got big doses of his teaching as well, which was in my opinion invaluable. Calle had a funny habit, by the way, of unconsciously miming any scene he happened to be watching. He would mime every word to himself with all the appropriate facial expressions of sorrow, anger, irony, quite unknown to himself. He had a strong sense of leadership, but was never intimidating. He was one of us, and just as childish. His laughter was infectious, and though he was a mine of information what he told us took on the quality of a fairytale. There was nothing professorial about him and he was always an exhilarating experience.

Everything that was good in me he brought out and all the bad bits we threw away together. I began to get confidence; for the first time I dared to look at the world and myself and feel I had a place in it. There were actually four of us under-privileged girls who had quit school at about fourteen, whom Calle was helping by giving free lessons. When we came to him we didn't expect much from the world, if anything at all; we had already been very hurt by it. Calle changed all that; he made us believe we could fit, but first we had to change ourselves and therefore be part of changing life patterns in a changing world.

Imagine a sombre, narrow street in the heart of the city, which now of course has been torn down to make way for modern office blocks and five-storey car-parks. Calle and his mother lived on the first floor of a saffron-coloured, solid-looking building where everything smelt clean, proper, very Swedish: that is, it had no smell at all. But when the door was opened by Calle's mother you entered another world, and were met with other smells. Her appearance was not exactly typical of a mother of a drama teacher in Stockholm. She would be wearing Calle's long underwear pinned to his grey socks, a pair of well-worn plimsolls, and a three-quarter length dress in some kind of black print which reminds me now of the material worn by little old ladies in Provence. She obviously cared about the neck-line because pinned to the dress would be

ora Robson in a performance of The *ncing Girl at the Academy of Dramatic Art in 1920.*

Robert Morley in Major Barbara *(1940), one of his first films, in which he played Undershaft. On the left is Rex Harrison.*

Lilli Palmer.   (I.T.C.)

Dulcie Gray.

Patrick Macnee in a 1951 performance of
The Rivals.

Yvonne Mitchell.

little lace frills, which she would change every so often. The only other coquettish streak in her manifested itself in her hair. Every morning she would light a small spirit lamp and heat curling-irons on it and do her own hair-dressing. Over the years she had singed quite badly the little curls round her forehead, so they were slightly yellow in comparison with her otherwise silver-grey hair. The finishing touch was the big fat cigar that dangled at the corner of her mouth. I never saw her without it, lit or unlit. It was just there, like an extension of herself. She could be friendly, she could be tough, she could be in a bad temper if anyone had dared to annoy Calle. Then she would sit down at a little upright piano and bang out some Wagner very loudly so that no one should hear him grumbling. She loved him more than her own life, and in his fashion he adored her just as much. They were inseparable; they teased and laughed at each other, and would have long arguments about contemporary writers on ballet, music and the arts in general. Calle was an inspired talker, and his mother was not half bad either, but she could be malicious, too, and tell killing stories about some of the people she didn't much care for. But hers was a very special brand of humour, and the glint in her eye was basically kind. The fact that she was Danish explained a lot of that side of her temperament.

To reach Calle you had to go down a long passage whose walls were covered with old stage portraits, big dog-eared posters and theatre programmes, all yellowed with age and cigar smoke. Then you would pass a kitchen door that no one —not even Calle—was allowed to enter; it was Mother's domain. Then finally you'd find the place where Calle resided —a rather large but gloomy room enveloped in a constant cloud of cigar smoke, whose walls were just as cluttered as those of the passage, and rich in memories of Calle's efforts as an actor in his early days, even though they hadn't been too successful. And there he would be, larger than life, puffing, grunting, holding forth, dancing to Mother's music, showing some of his steps—which didn't vary very much—for one of the operetta scenes. He would be dressed in a sort of brownish-grey suit which had somehow turned a funny mouldy colour in various places. He would have on a stiff white collar which he would sometimes throw off (to Mother's annoyance) when he got a bit too excited. Finally he too had the inevitable cigar, always in his mouth. He would hardly ever sit down or sit still unless we had a very serious scene to play.

Sometimes he would wear a curious large chequered dressing-gown whose colour for the life of me I couldn't describe, and an old red fez with a dangling tassel—a strange outfit for a rather over-sized man. I suppose Calle and his mother could be called dirty and messy, but somehow it never worried us. They were different, they were loving, they gave us all they had in every possible way, and not only did we not pay, but we were constantly being taken out for little meals. I think it was the first time I ever went to a restaurant; although it was a very humble one, I was deeply impressed. And later, when we had flown away from the nest, as it were, they always kept in touch by letter, sending press cuttings and asking us out for dinner so that we could talk, though on the whole it was only Calle's voice that was heard. But we were grateful, we lapped it up; we needed his enthusiasm, we had not experienced such a thing before. And I'm glad to remember that we were really appreciative, and did not take it for granted—which could have been very easy, I suppose, as they both spoilt us.

We never knew quite how to show our gratitude, but once I remember we gave Mother a perhaps rather unsuitable Christmas present. Her handbag was falling apart, only held together by a rubber band, so we decided it was about time she had a new one. It was fire-engine red, in shining plastic. She was very proud of it, although it didn't fit in with the rest of her. We felt we had made a mistake, but 'Oh, no,' she said, 'it was *positive*.' (Calle always wore a button on his lapel saying 'Be an optimist'.) But one day we really had an opportunity to do something for her. We had come to school to find her

crying, which was quite a shock, and she told us that they had
to leave the flat because the building was going to be demolished.
'It's impossible,' she kept on crying. 'Why?' we asked, not
understanding. 'Oh, all the boxes,' she said. We had never
seen any boxes. All we had seen was a chaise longue and a
rocking chair, a few odds and ends for changing our scenery in
the sketches—and all the photographs, of course. 'What boxes?'
we asked. She just pointed at the kitchen door, and started to
cry again.

After much persuasion we got her to accept our offer to go
into the kitchen and help clean it out. We didn't know what
we had let ourselves in for! Certainly it was an experience not
to be missed. Among the débris it contained we encountered
the remains of four birthday parties. Over the year we were
always lavishly treated to cream cakes and chocolate and
whipped cream on our birthdays; well, here were the left-overs,
now rotting in cartons. In the sink the cups were floating in a
mouldy layer of cream and chocolate, and everywhere there
were cigar butts. We admitted to feeling a bit queasy at the
first sight of it all, but we went to work. In the middle of the
room we discovered a filthy old armchair and some blankets—
on which we were to learn that Mother slept—surrounded by
hundreds of coloured shirts, collars, socks, and boxes and boxes
of odds and ends and bric-a-brac. I think we kept at it for
almost a week before it was eventually cleared out. And every
day we had a birthday party—Mother insisted that we be paid
in cream cakes and hot chocolate. It was difficult to work
amongst the odd socks and cigar butts while outside Calle was
firing away his instructions, his temper flying as Mother
wasn't at hand, yet never once did he enter the kitchen. I think
he pretended it didn't exist, since he never mentioned our
helping Mother pack, only showed great surprise at seeing us at
unaccustomed times.

From time to time Mother would become worried about
Calle's sex life. One evening she had gone down the street and
picked up a pretty girl and left her alone with Calle for more

than an hour. She crept back, and hearing Calle's voice, decided she could go in. There he was, declaiming a fairytale by Hans Christian Andersen, whom he loved. The girl sat at his feet, her face flooded with tears. Later on that girl became quite a successful pupil.

The following summer I was working with Calle and the little group at the Tivoli outside Stockholm. We did a children's matinee performance on the big open stage in between jugglers and trapeze artists. We were ecstatic, we sang and danced scenes from *The Wizard of Oz*, and Calle told a fairytale. We worked for next to nothing and a card that gave us free rides on the roller coasters, the big wheel, all the attractions, even the rifle range and the china-breaking booth. We really got to know the ins and outs of the fairground, and made friends with the giant lady with the beard, though our great heroine was the beautiful Indian snakecharmer—I don't know how many performances we watched.

After that summer we wanted to change our profession. The theatre seemed dull and tame in comparison with the circus; I dreamt about circus life, of becoming a clown. After a few talks with one, however, I grew very down-hearted. I was told there was no tradition of female clowns. I had heard that sentence before! So, I carried on with Calle. I took up singing with him and found I had a strong voice; at least there was a tradition there for women. With Calle conducting and humming and Mother banging out the tunes on the upright, I sang Gluck, I sang Schubert, I sang Carmen and folk songs. It was my first real contact with music and I was on a cloud.

That autumn I and another girl from our select group got an engagement in a rather seedy night-club called The Bluebird, smack opposite the National Theatre. We were billed as Mai and Boj, Two Swedish Nightingales in Rosita Serrano style (at that time the Portuguese singer was a great favourite with Swedes). We were dressed in some kind of Austrian outfit— heaven knows why—flowered skirts and dainty little aprons: a pair of Lolitas, we had trouble almost from the start. So

Calle and his mother decided to sit through each of the two performances at night, as both a protection and an inspiration.

What was it, then, that Calle offered us, that was so unique and so different from what I was to encounter when I joined the National Theatre School? First, perhaps, a great sense of adventure and an acute awareness of ourselves; then, love and affection and a home. His enthusiasm infected us, he had excitement and joy. He gave us that thing called security, and last but certainly not least, he believed in us utterly. What a difference then to encounter an Institution, a temple of stone, a monument to the arts—the National Theatre in Stockholm. However well-meaning, it was cold and sterile, it could never be a home. Such an institution can't compete with a great personality who needs freedom to survive, who has a great vision, and who lives and eats and sleeps his passion.

One day a friend told me she was going to try to get into the National Theatre School which had a three-year course and a great reputation. Both Garbo and the two great Bergmans, Ingmar and Ingrid, were connected with it. It was the ultimate for an actor in Sweden, the holiest of holies; it scared me, it intimidated me, it made me feel insecure, yet I said I too would try my luck. Why shouldn't I? I took with me three scenes that I had done with Calle, *Easter* by Strindberg, *Mädchen in Uniform*, and a Shakespeare play. I didn't dare tell Calle about it, I felt quite dreadful when I filled in the form. How could I do this to him? I took my courage and a Bible and I entered that monumental place with fear in my heart. After the second test, however, I was still among those selected for the third and last test. There were only twenty left out of a hundred. And I made it, and so did the other girl. It was unbelievable.

I immediately rushed to tell Calle. He was not a bit upset, of course, but overjoyed, and took us out for a celebration dinner, and told everybody about us like some proud father. I still had a week of my contract to do at The Bluebird, and one night to my great horror I saw all the front tables were taken by the great directors of the National Theatre and the Principal herself.

I got a stipendium and I started at the school. It was certainly different. I had entered a grand Institution, with its sacred Green Room. How awed I was as I slunk around, eyes downcast! The only place I dared to sit was on the bench with the galoshes and boots, half hidden among the fur coats and the black woollen cape of Lars Hanson, the great actor whom we all adored and revered, and who scared the life out of us. A lone wolf, he would stalk the corridors, and in the Green Room where the other actors read the daily papers and gossiped or listened to the radio in between their entrances, he was unapproachable, aloof and in his own world; he continued to live his part. I would watch him with awe, sensing the concentration around him like a sacred circle. I think I learnt more from just watching him offstage than I learnt in the school itself. I admired his skill with the spittoon which was at one end of the Green Room, into which he would spit with great contempt, just missing the top of the head of another actor idly gossiping nearby.

I was timid. I didn't fit in. At eighteen, I was the youngest in the school. I became silent and withdrawn—the mouse once again. My class-mates were well-read and academic. I was self-educated. I had no manners, no culture. I was nothing, I decided. Feeling inferior, I became stupid and could never answer any questions in the classes on the history of the theatre. Instead I excelled when it came to the acting itself. We had lessons in dance, deportment, voice technique; at none was I any good. The boys could do fencing—I envied them. I was not allowed to because I was a girl—yes, there it was again, no tradition for women in fencing, the fencemaster said. But there were some good things in the National Theatre at that time, which I believe have now been eliminated. For one thing, the students were allowed to take part as extras in the big productions of Alf Sjöberg and Olof Molander, the two great directors of the Theatre in those days. They were talented, they were exciting, they were demanding, but they were totally different from Calle. They were domineering, and they could be cruel, though they did teach me much of what I know about the theatre. Day after day we had time to watch their work, and also the work of the great actors. I began to read in order to catch up on my scanty education.

It was difficult for me to communicate. The only way I managed it successfully was on the stage, and after one year I got a big and unusual chance: a lead in the Maxwell Anderson play, *The Eve of St Mark*, and it was an instant success. After that I hardly attended any classes at the school, but had big parts in Shakespeare productions, and then I played in Sartre, Lorca and Strindberg.

So, I had become a successful actress at the age of nineteen. Calle glowed; it was his success too, he said. Again and again I found myself going to him for guidance, for security. When I got a leading part opposite Lars Hanson, my idol, I quivered with fright and it was Calle who reassured me and gave me the strength to stand up to the extraordinary power of that very great actor. The play we did was *Shadow and Substance*, by an Irish writer called Paul Vincent Carrol. The play was a success, and the sparks flew between Lars Hanson and myself, but I don't think somehow I would have been able to match up to that genius had it not been for Calle. 'Trust yourself,' he said, 'be true to yourself, be open. Dare to stand up for yourself, no matter what, and dare to change. Never allow yourself to become too settled. Learn that there is no security.' That's why when, three years later, I got the chance to go to London to make a film, I could gladly and freely give up the National Theatre, despite the screams of horror that arose. 'You're mad!'—'You don't know what you're going into!'—'What if you're not a success?'

However, I left and I have not regretted it. How could I? Life is change—and as the philosophers say, it's better to live in a state of impermanence than in one of finality.

Yes, Calle, you had a lot of rough edges, you would not have fitted into the National Theatre, you would have died a slow death there. You taught me that it is better to be free than secure, and you believed in the value of change.

So, when fifteen years later I decided I'd had enough of acting, I would become a film director, and once again I heard the objection that had been raised so many times before—that there was no tradition of women film-makers—I told myself what Calle would have said: 'Go ahead, change, you have the right just as much as anyone else. Anyway, why not start a new tradition?'

Ann Jellicoe

Ann Jellicoe is a playwright who intended to be a theatrical director, and still prefers directing to any other form of theatre work. But having won a prize in the Observer *Playwriting Competition of 1956 she was, she says, labelled a playwright and instantly accepted into the Royal Court Theatre at its most exciting period. Five of her six plays have been produced at the Court. She has also written children's plays and made translations* (Rosmersholm, The Lady From the Sea, The Seagull, Der Freischutz). *Her best known work is probably* The Knack *which briefly swept her into a glamorous and precarious world where a test of success is a good table at Sardi's. But* The Knack *was an expensive play in emotional terms, being the outcome of a bitter period of her life and she has not, she says, been driven to that degree of comedy again.*

She now lives a turbulent life in Dorset with her photographer husband Roger Mayne and their two children.

y mother came from the north, my father from the south and out of their conflicts came I. My parents separated when I was eighteen months old and my eyes began to cross: if a young child is put under too much strain the tension will erupt at a weak spot, in my case eyes. Sometimes the child develops a stammer. From then on I had to wear glasses. A man is leaving his wife; but if he has a young daughter he is telling her too that the most important man in her life does not value her and, by association, she is not attractive to men. Such wounds don't heal but at least they provide some of the energy by which I write.

At four years old I was sent to a kindergarten and there, in a play, I was cast as Sleeping Beauty. Even after forty-five years the whole image of that performance hangs in my mind. I got hooked on theatre. All through childhood I remained perfectly sure of what I wanted to do. At eight years old I was sent to a girls' boarding-school; when not actually in class we were left more or less alone and unsupervised with predictable results. It may have been happy accident which led me to organize the others into getting up small shows and plays. Why didn't they resent the bossing and organization it entailed? But they were grateful: instead of hunting each other in packs it gave them something positive to do. I found I could deflect hurt through theatre and gain, if not power, then a means of controlling my surroundings; if not popularity, then a kind of acceptance and recognition.

By the time I was fourteen it was accepted that if something theatrical was required they could turn to me. The shows I got up were not like the school play: Shakespeare and such rehearsed over a whole term. They were glorified charades, meant to last half an hour or so and, by their very nature, not scripted. If something was wanted I lay awake in bed, where you could be quite certain of not being interrupted, and worked it all out. In an hour or so of intense concentration the whole thing would be organized in my head: structure, story, characters, dialogue. Nothing was written down. Next day I told everyone what they had to say and do and we got on with rehearsing it. It was an amazing discipline in basic theatre: it taught me that theatre can be created under the simplest conditions using only actors, audience and ideas.

For many years I never officially admitted that I wanted to be an actress. Perhaps the very word explains why. Instead I gave out that I was going to be an architect, the profession of an admired uncle, and thus avoided fatuous questions and explanations. All through childhood one was conditioned to do as one was told; or rather once in boarding-school there were few choices to be made. Both I and my parents did what the school required: they paid the bills, I turned up on the first day of term in correct uniform with my lacrosse stick strapped to my suitcase. This went on until school narrowed and certain choices had to be made between say, mathematics and extra elocution (which they called 'diction', a more neutral word). Then I saw that I must state plainly that I wanted to go into the theatre or I would get the wrong training.

Once the announcement had been made it was clear that opposition to the idea had existed only in my own head. My father said: 'You don't want to go to 'varsity then?' (His word.) And I began to see how all barriers to action had been built, if not by me, then with my connivance. I wrote off to the two best known drama schools and arranged a visit to London for interviews. The field was open: I was free. The independence was more apparent than real: Father paid, he had always done so and I never questioned it. I hope it is not ungrateful to say that it was probably his class-sense: it would

have seemed to him a reflection on his status and virility not to
have provided for his daughter. I was lucky: my grandmother's
generation won for women the right to work, but my father
was still sufficiently Edwardian to make me an allowance.

The chief dramatic establishments were then the Royal
Academy of Dramatic Art and the Central School of Speech
Training and Dramatic Art. It was 1945 and both were somewhat rundown. Staffing must have been devilish, there were
almost no male teachers or students, everyone was tired; the
schools were running on residual momentum. RADA, founded
in 1904 by Beerbohm Tree, was supposed to be the more down
to earth and practical. I auditioned into a black void to, I
suppose, the principal Sir Kenneth Barnes who had held a
comfy roost there since 1909. RADA presumably liked the
look of me because I was offered a place; but what was I
supposed to make of them? Having been conditioned by
boarding-school not to make a fuss or ask awkward questions
I don't suppose I even formulated my doubts in my own mind
but, feeling slightly dissatisfied, trotted off to Central to have a
look there.

The Central School was curiously housed in the thickness of
the Albert Hall. This amazing structure—Britannia's reply to
the Roman Coliseum—has an outer shell about 30 feet wide,
sliced into five or six levels and honeycombed with passages,
lobbies, crush and refreshment rooms, lavatories, offices, royal
retiring rooms, organ pipes, store and sluice rooms. The whole
threaded through by staircases: some leading to side exits on
the ground floor, others plunging on to lower regions where,
beyond the boiler rooms and burrowed beneath the organ, was
the musicians' refreshment room: an Edwardian survival,
warm and humid, smelling of tea and gas. Most of the time the
whole building was sunk into an intense stillness and crepusc-
ular gloom. The great passages, wide enough for two Centuries
to pass, curled away into gathering blackness which, if one had
to go the long way round, became tangible as one walked into
it (keeping a slightly circular course), one's flesh prickling. A

wedge of this colossal gâteau housed the Central School, and while it would be untrue to say that you can always tell a Central student because he can't walk in a straight line, the oval structure of the Albert Hall was a curious place in which to train drama students, and may have contributed to the School's womanish air.

I forget whether I auditioned (in an oddity of a theatre more or less fully equipped and set within the same inner arc), but recall a strong impression of my interview and first meeting with Gwynneth Thurburn who was to become a steady influence over the next ten years. Thurb is a woman you do not miss: tall and sometimes seeming exhausted by her height; grey hair, short but·not severe; one eye darting, the other fixed: a grand, innocent, ramshackle air about her. She had a baffling devotion to Central. I have never known anyone in such a position with less personal ambition. But she held Central together during the war, pulled it up afterwards and, when the lease at the Albert Hall was due to run out and the school in danger of fading away, she somehow found the money and will to shift to new and permanent premises. With the unblunted arrogance of youth I took her modesty, kindness and loyalty for granted and relied on them. She almost never imposed herself but once or twice she gave me a terrific shock when she intervened at certain key moments of my life with dramatic emphasis.

Central had been founded by Elsie Fogerty who was a product of the craft movement of the 1880s and who probably owed a good deal to William Poel. Poel had revolutionized the speaking of Shakespearian verse, substituting a light, rapid, highly-inflected style for the ponderous delivery of the old actors. In his semi-professional productions (Edith Evans was still a milliner when she worked with him), Poel tended to use women in men's parts: they were easier to get hold of and more docile. Elsie Fogerty had also helped establish the University of London Diploma in Dramatic Art. The Central School was suffused with these three qualities: a proudly emphatic speech training (this was their speciality), a slightly pseudo academicism and an air of mild lesbianism. It was reassuringly like school so I chose to go there.

When I arrived the Central School was probably near its lowest ebb. The training we received was very conventional, harking back to 1920 or even 1910. The teachers were a mixed bunch. The atmosphere could have been called relaxed and easy-going or merely tired and sloppy, and by today's standards the students were not worked nearly hard enough. This can be demoralizing: in my second year I began to skip classes on quite a scale because I found them boring and considered I had better things to do. Such carryings on in a student today would enrage me; but it may be quite a good atmosphere in which to develop certain kinds of talent and an immature personality. One was left to grow in one's own way and at one's own pace. Certain things we did actually learn: voice training was very thorough, the means seem archaic now. We had bone props which we set between our teeth for tongue and lip exercises; they became foul and grubby and in time were lost; no one seemed to care: perhaps by that time you had caught the habit of keeping your jaw open when speaking. Boarding-school had quickly knocked the Yorkshire 'wŏn' for 'one' out of me. Now Central corrected the over-genteel: I said 'Alice has a rabbit' in voice exercises instead of 'Elice hes a rebbit'. Over three years they aimed to teach vocal control, flexibility, clarity and resonance. Even today I retain crumbs of that technique and find them useful. We did a good deal of verse speaking (Thurb's speciality), which is good for an interpretive artist; amongst other things it teaches artistic humility. We did plays in which I, being a big girl, was landed with men's parts. It was not, on the whole, inspired teaching and I jogged along as I had done at school: not questioning too much but slowly sinking into a kind of boredom.

If Central sometimes seemed a bit flat one's social life, outside the school, grew steadily more interesting as the year progressed. While still at boarding-school I had fixed myself up with a room in a hostel on Central's recommended list: two meals a day and three on Sundays for thirty shillings a week (they were awful meals); all in by ten o'clock unless you signed the late book, last in chain the door. No men. I had never been so happy in my life. For nine years I had lived a communal and over-organized routine; now I had a room of my own, a gas ring and time of my own. If today I find myself threading the dusty canyons of South Kensington, scuffing dead leaves along the pavements, the spice of that autumn rises up.

After three months in the hostel, just long enough for the first ecstasy to subside, I was invited to make a fifth in what was for the time a rather classy mansion flat: I believe Princess Alice lived two floors up. One of the girls in the group was a natural honey blonde, frilly as a pink carnation. Her immense train of admirers, squashed eyeball to eyeball in the tiny, clattering lift or trying to corner her in the hall away from the other chaps in the sitting-room, were quite glad really to take one of the other girls to a party just so long as they were near Kitty. I already had a sort of boy friend: a student from the Royal School of Mines, but Kitty's taste was for officers, and more particularly Guards Officers. Most men were in uniform at that time and the flat swarmed with representatives of His Majesty's Armed Forces. Checking her clothing coupons one day Kitty gave an enchanting sigh: 'Even if we don't have dresses,' she said, 'at least we have officers.' The word 'have' was used in its strictly limited sense, nothing could have been more virginal. Five girls, four bedrooms, endless men and not one fuck. At that time girls of my class and background went so far and no further or they kept very quiet about it. All the same the fun and games had its effect on our work and even the Central School took notice. At the end of the year the flat broke up when two of the girls were chucked out, one was transferred to another course. Kitty was 'warned' but kept on because they clearly thought she was going to be a film star.

I decided not to go back to the hostel but to look for an

unfurnished flat of my own. This was greeted with some scepticism by my family since flats were then as dew in the Sahara. But what with my glasses and the actress's dodge of dressing the part I must have looked reassuring because I was offered two flats within two hours. I settled on the top floor of an old house in Pimlico: two rooms and a kitchen, and lived there for twenty-five shillings a week, rising to twenty-seven when a bath was installed in the lavatory two floors down. With Father's allowance, this tiny cheap flat and virtually no responsibilities I was free as I have never been before or since. The flat had no front door and sometimes I would scarcely bother to lock up but simply walked the three minutes down the road to Victoria, caught the cross-channel ferry and stayed abroad with friends for as long as I felt like it. I would return to find the dirty cup and saucer where I had left them three months before, and my allowance gently accumulating in the bank. I appreciated my good fortune and used it. I was a boarding-school child and today such children are often called 'privileged': I think they are seriously deprived and may well become emotional cripples. But six years of economic and emotional freedom, work you like and foreign travel: that is privilege.

In this flat I started my second year at Central. It was a three-year course and really far too long for its content. In point of fact I did a lot of useful work: consolidating and developing, and beginning to direct other students in productions which went well. But all the same I had a nasty sense of losing momentum. To be fair I don't think it was all the fault of the course: it may have been part of a natural and familiar process common to artists, and mystics. It would have been inflated to call this mood 'The Dark Night of the Soul', but there was depression and loss of direction, the work seemed pointless and unrewarding.

There was a further unsettling development in 1946 when the Old Vic School was formed under Michel St Denis. This was a reincarnation of his pre-war London Theatre Studio and

was to become by far the most important and effective of the
immediate post-war drama schools. St Denis was the nephew
of Jacques Copeau and had passed through the ferment of the
Vieux Colombier and the European experimental theatre of the
'thirties. With him were George Devine and Glen Byam Shaw:
all three were dynamic men, just returned from the war and
bursting to work in the theatre again. Although the post-war
theatre was not innovatory—that had to wait ten years—the
Old Vic School was twenty years ahead of the others: it was
fresh, vigorous and masculine. To get the school going they
rather unscrupulously offered a shortened course to drama
students already in training and many Central and RADA
students were enticed away. I didn't go, partly because I felt it
would be disloyal to Central (which betrays my insecurity),
but mostly because I was too self-absorbed to appreciate what
was happening and its importance. I would have been wise to
go to the Old Vic School: their training was far better and
they had their own outlets into the professional theatre. But in
fact their influence spread so quickly it was impossible to avoid.
Later, as a teacher, I absorbed a great deal from a colleague
who had worked with St Denis, and of course I came to know
the ideas and methods of George Devine and Glen Byam Shaw
very well indeed.

About this time Central made it possible for me to work with
the 'Compagnie des Quinze' who were visiting London with
La Maison de Bernarda Alba. They hadn't bothered to bring
over the actors for their bit parts which, knowing their methods,
were probably played by the sweepings of the theatre anyway.
Thus my first, paid, professional appearance was in French.
And it was a very curious experience. Our first, and just about
only, rehearsal was *siffler*. We don't have precisely this practice
in England: the company sat round a table and whispered
through the play at terrific speed. Somehow we three students
caught our cues, delivered our five or six words, and the play
rushed on. It was ruthlessly professional, and there was a sense
of the French tradition behind it: I am sure Molière's company

would have used this method to slot an old play back into the repertory. They were full of the old tricks and compromises of theatre practice. *The House of Bernarda Alba* has an all-female cast but, when a crowd of peasants filed on for a funeral, shrouded in black from head to foot, anything in the theatre on two legs was hidden under a costume and pushed onstage. Towards the end of the first performance the stage manager led us to the back of the stalls and we were thrilled to realize that we were to be a claque. The actresses had the French mixture of amiability and edge. They were a friendly lot: someone possessed a ravishing little black hat which was passed around the company according to need; only when we went to the French Embassy for afternoon tea (with whisky) could you assume that the hat had come to rest on the head of its rightful owner.

With all this going on how could I be dull? But youth is bloody-minded. I now heard that a friend was going to stay with a Swiss family to polish up her French. It sounded fun so I went too. In point of fact this visit cleared up my depression, led to one of the most lasting friendships of my life and, by means too devious to relate here, I acquired Swedish which later brought in cash and kudos. But at the time it must have seemed, if not actually insane, then grossly irresponsible towards my work and the Central School. Any student carrying on now as I did then would have been pushed out months before. Indeed later when I was teaching, and discipline was much stricter, a group of students, among them Vanessa Redgrave, had the temerity to overstay their visit to Spain by three days: they were studying Lorca and at the last minute had discovered the village where he had lived. They received a very strong reprimand indeed. I don't know if it was faith in talent or a technique of negative encouragement, easily mistaken for sloppiness, which led Central to let me get away with it.

When I returned for the last few months of my final year everything began to unlock. The quite considerable amount of work I had previously done began to serve a free-flowing artistic energy and, in a series of hurdles leading up to the Final Show, I began to find my stride. At some festival or other I had an important breakthrough when speaking poetry. I had spent nearly six months studying Keats's 'Ode to a Nightingale' and towards the end was disciplined and delicate in allowing the poem to come gently to fullness. At the moment of performance I had the transcendent experience of the poem speaking itself, of being far beyond intellect or technique, of being merely a vessel through which something was revealed. It was probably my first, and certainly my first conscious, experience of inspiration. I began to understand artistic truth and how one may try to achieve it.

About this time Christopher Fry, who was then only just becoming known for his first, short play, *A Phoenix Too Frequent*, was invited to give playwriting classes to the acting students. Today this would be normal stuff at, say, Dartington College of Arts; but in 1947 it reveals a certain freedom of thought in Thurb. I must say if I were now asked to give actors a playwriting course I would refuse the job as impossible. Maybe Fry needed the money, but actually the classes had some value. He must have been very practical in his approach; I have never forgotten two extremely sensible remarks: 'Never have a meal onstage'. Very sound advice: meals are hell for stage management and for actors trying to make themselves heard through mouthfuls of bread soggy with gravy browning. And the director has setting problems: either someone sits throughout the scene with his back to the audience masking everyone else or you have a bizarre seating plan. Fry's second maxim appears equally explicit but is in fact much more subtle: 'Never have a scene with only two characters'. Dialogue between two actors can become lifeless, you must think of the rhythm of a scene. He started me thinking about pace, rhythm and climax in the theatre. I have sometimes broken this rule but never forgotten the point behind it.

Having now her tame playwright, Thurb was not slow to

use him. The war in Europe was over and they were trying to make a start with clearing away the rubble; there was a sense that somehow life must be coaxed back to normal. Central decided that this year there must be a *public* Final Show. This was to take place at the Globe Theatre, Shaftesbury Avenue and the program of short scenes would include an extract from a new and unfinished work by Christopher Fry. During rehearsal he decided he would call it: *The Lady's Not For Burning*, which we thought was a very nice title. We had to audition for parts. Two of us read for the lead; my rival was an attractive girl who read well. All I could see in the part was its sexiness and my confidence deserted me; my reading was appalling: false and flirtatious. At this point Thurb made one of her climactic interventions: 'Ann must read again,' she said. So I got the part. It was tough on the other girl but she was not one to be cast down. I won the Elsie Fogerty Prize but hadn't the sense or confidence to take advantage of it. Penny got a job at the Old Vic by stuffing her bra with socks when they said she was too immature to play the widow in *The Taming of the Shrew*.

After I left Central I did a spell in provincial rep and then worked sporadically as an actress and stage manager. Television, with its insatiable demand, had not yet got going. Brecht had still to teach us that actresses need not always be pretty. The lack of work irritated me and so, having done some research into theatre architecture and become interested in the Open Stage, I started an experimental theatre club. There were then no Arts Council grants and I did it by writing round to my friends and asking them for half a crown subscription. The simplicity of the scheme was a logical development of my previous experience. We used professional actors and gave Sunday performances. Even today the Royal Court theatre with all its prestige finds it difficult to cast Sunday shows; but at that time there was little television and actors were trapped in long runs with very little to do; even so casting was my biggest problem. The Cockpit Club was the first of the English

Open Stage theatres, and for it I wrote one or two short plays and made my first translations. Amazingly we ended up with a profit; the first show cost £17 and made £25; we spent £25 on the second and made £30, and so on; in the end there was £18 in the bank. Today one would have been able to get a substantial grant and with such money I think I could have lifted the Cockpit Club onto a secure and regular footing. But as it was, after two years of intensely hard work, Thurb asked me to go back to Central to teach acting and I was glad to accept.

By the time I returned Central had been transformed: there had been a big turnover in staff and there was now a reasonable proportion of men students. The acting course was much more efficiently structured, due mostly to Oliver Reynolds who was Head of Drama in all but name. (Walter Hudd, the actor, had the title.) Oliver is one of the most influential teachers I have known. He is a passionately austere man whose authority derives partly from natural gift but also from his air of detachment and a strong sense of irony. He has a trick of reflecting back one's foolishness so that if, faltering under his questioning eye, I said something stupid he would pause and murmur, 'Really ducky?' and an abyss of fatuity gaped at one's feet. I admired his work immensely and worked with him closely for two years but I was not one of those who knew him intimately: his cool, ironic manner kept one at arm's length. So I can only guess at why he has never gone into the professional theatre where his talent would certainly equal the best of his contemporaries. He would seem to be one of those people who, given independent means, are firm-minded enough to run their lives rather than letting life run them.

Oliver had studied under Michel St Denis and then become one of the teachers at his school (as did George Devine and Glen Byam Shaw) so he brought their methods, ideas and standards to the Central School and transformed that fubsy old knitting shop into something much tougher. This was 1953, and for all the originality of his ideas he had a rigid streak which might not be popular today. I can imagine his blistering sarcasm at some student wanting to organize his own course. But at a time when Central needed a firm hand he gave it; of the students, some worshipped, some hated but—by God!— they all respected him. I learned immensely from him, observing his work whenever I could: I still follow his meticulous method of preparing a director's script. I was dazzled by the boldness of his productions. Under the surface of his logic, analysis, control there was also passion: it came out in his productions and also in his occasional anger; and this gave him humanity and vitality. I had always had a fairly firm intuition as to what made good acting and good theatre, but through teaching, and through association with Oliver Reynolds, I began to organize, articulate and justify my opinions.

I continued to be financially secure. I was now married and whereas before I lived off Father I now lived off my husband. I took it for granted; nowadays one would be too aware. If you were strong-minded and, possibly, selfish enough, there were advantages at that time to being a woman. Because of this support I had been able to run the Cockpit Club and so begin to explore new physical resources of theatre. Now I could take a badly-paid job at Central where one was exposed to seminal ideas and had time to think. One day I was watching one of Oliver's students improvising: he was playing a trumpet and it turned into a bird and flew away. Such freedom would be common today but, in 1954, watching that image develop, I suddenly felt, amidst all the welter of ideas and impressions crowding and shouting at one, that this was something tangible and strong. The germ of an idea of theatre not poetic, symbolist or literary: a theatre of direct action and concrete images. The *Observer* playwriting competition was announced. I gave up the job at Central and wrote *The Sport of My Mad Mother* in which, as I now see, it is all there: the primitive hunting packs of school, the confidence that theatre can be achieved by the simplest means, Fry's remarks on rhythm, Oliver's freedom of images, and much more. And so one was swept into a wider and more boisterous sea.

Peter Sallis

Peter Sallis was born at Twickenham in 1921. He worked in a bank for a couple of years before enlisting in the RAF for the war years. After demobilization he won a Scholarship to RADA, where he was a student from 1946–8. His work in the theatre began with a production of The Scheming Lieutenant *by Sheridan at the Arts Theatre in London. From 1948 until the present day he has been in and out of the West End, appearing in some interesting productions such as the Gielgud season at the Lyric, Hammersmith; Orson Welles'* productions of Moby Dick *and* Rhinoceros (*the latter with Olivier*); *three musicals* (*one of them*, Baker Street, *on Broadway*); *the thriller* Wait Until Dark *at the Strand Theatre;* Inadmissible Evidence (*also on Broadway*).

He has worked almost continuously on television since 1952, and among the series he has worked in are The Diary of Samuel Pepys *and* Last of the Summer Wine. *He has also appeared in a number of films, including* Anastasia, The VIP's, Saturday Night and Sunday Morning, Inadmissible Evidence, *and* The Incredible Sarah.

Looking back, I cannot be sure which year the war stopped. Was it 1945? Both of them? The German and the Japanese? I remember reading about the atom bomb from the headlines of a newspaper in the Course Hut of No. 1 Radio School, Cranwell. I had very little knowledge of radio and even less of atoms: it was simply all over. I had contributed about as much to winning it as our dog. But it had acted as a catalyst; the war, that is. I had done some acting at Cranwell under the friendly and eagle eye of Leslie Sands and had decided to become a professional actor instead of returning to the job which I was doing before the war, bank clerk. ('Barclays, Bloomsbury,' I found it difficult to say this when answering the telephone.)

Another friend of mine in the Air Force had taken me into his confidence and explained that I had only one quality and that was an ability to amuse people. But I knew that I had another requisite that makes people become actors for money: I wanted to be recognized. I wanted to be 'someone', however small. This is not a quality to be admired but it seems to be a built-in ingredient of the acting fraternity. I had done no acting at school. I had not been in the school play but I did think I might be good at it; an instinctive thought encouraged by my job as a teacher in the RAF. There is a connection between acting and teaching as there is between acting and the law.

I was lucky enough to know in the mid-'forties Daphne Banks, a daughter of Leslie Banks, the distinguished actor. (Daphne had married a colleague of mine at Cranwell, Peter Gough, a man of enormous personality and talent.) At that time Leslie Banks was playing in John Gielgud's company at the Theatre Royal, Haymarket. I went one matinee of *A Midsummer Night's Dream* with an introduction from Daphne to see her father. He gave me two pieces of advice; to read Stanislavsky's *An Actor Prepares* and to go to the Royal Academy of Dramatic Art. I bought the book on my way back to Cranwell and, as soon as I was able, I filled in the form for an audition to RADA.

Because I was in uniform I was allowed to enter for the Alexander Korda scholarship. Sir Alexander Korda was nearly a genius. Not only did he make outstanding films (*Rembrandt*, *Henry the Eighth*), but he made them in England and he made them with Charles Laughton. With some of the money that his films provided he subsidised a number of scholarships to RADA for people serving in the armed forces. It meant that people like myself who might not otherwise have been able to afford it had their fees paid. A small allowance was provided additionally. Nowadays the State pays for everything but in those days grants were not known. Without the scholarship I doubt if I could have gone. At this distance of time the only other names I can remember who were also Korda scholars were Eric Lander, Julia Jones (now a writer) and Emrys Leyshon. But in all there were about six or eight of us.

I was invited to the Academy to audition for the scholarship. I learned three pieces: Benedick from *Much Ado about Nothing* (based upon Donald Wolfit whom I did not resemble in the slightest); Trigorin in *The Three Sisters*; and one of the choruses from *Henry V*, an unwitting acknowledgment to Leslie Banks who had played the part in Olivier's film.

Before I went onto the stage for my audition I waited in the wings with a young man who, if he had leanings, would probably have preferred me to, say, Julia Jones. 'Are you

nervous?' he said. 'Yes,' I said. 'Breathe deeply,' he said. I
tried but it didn't help me any more then than it does today.
I did the audition, was asked if I could find my own way out,
and left about as certain as I could be that I had failed. When
I walked down Gower Street to my credit I thought that, having
failed, I would not give up the profession for which I believed I
was best suited. It is almost the only time in my life I can
remember feeling strong-minded.

As it happened I was accepted. Sir Kenneth Barnes, the
Principal, was kind enough to let me start straight away in
mid-term after my demob leave. I travelled daily from Leigh-
on-Sea via Fenchurch Street and the Central London line to
Gower Street, a journey of almost Dickensian proportions.
However, that was where my parents lived. I may have been
going into a fearsome profession but I was still a bank clerk at
heart. I had sent my mother and father, who were in the front
line, food parcels during the war. I was not going to desert
them now that it was all over.

Anybody who had so much as put on a uniform during the
war was treated with the greatest kindness by those who had
not. I found the atmosphere at the Academy in 1946 congenial,
sexy and serious. By sexy I don't mean the free-wheeling, free-
living attitude of mind that exists today. Simply·that if the
most dangerous thing that has happened to you during five
years of war is to fall off your bicycle in a race to see who can
get back to the NAAFI quickest, you can easily find yourself
pulled up short facing a semi-circle of nubile young ladies too
young to have suffered anything worse than evacuation to
Yeovil and all agape to find themselves facing a hero. I was
honest enough to admit that I had not shot down the Hermann
Goering circus but I was not going to tell them the whole truth.

Not everyone had as much faith in RADA as Leslie Banks.
I had heard that it was a finishing school for young ladies and
gentlemen; that you would develop a 'RADA' voice which
implied gentility and plumminess from Knightsbridge; that it
did not compare to gaining entry to a repertory company and

learning the hard way. At the time that I went there none of these disadvantages was apparent. To be fair, yes, there was a sprinkling of school-leavers but there was a leavening of older people. I was twenty-five and not the oldest. It may have been the aftermath of the war which had something to do with the prevailing atmosphere. The idea that it was over appealed to people. Even Churchill (I'm sure) was glad to be alive. So there was a prospect of a life ahead, a life to be lived for which some of us had been spared. Everyone responded to the challenge of starting life again, none more so than Sir Kenneth. The staff responded, the pupils responded. It was a good time to be there, I'm certain of it. The Academy may well have improved since then, but it had a special feeling about it in 1946 which I think would be hard to match.

Physically there was a hole in the middle of it. The original theatre had been hit by a bomb and there was a back to the Gower Street building which no architect had designed. You crossed the bombed-out space to reach Malet Street. Now the Vanbrugh Theatre stands in its place. Our theatre was a small rehearsal theatre which had been the number two before the bomb hit its companion. I remember the entrance hall, the offices and Sir Kenneth's room which were on the ground floor, the stone curved staircase which led to the classrooms on the upper floors, the canteen on the roof and the roof itself, a place to sun yourself and have your photo taken with your classmates. I imagine by today's standards the place was not very well equipped. I don't remember anyone grumbling. There was something approaching a students' union where pupils could air their views and grievances. I don't remember any of us taking much notice of it. We were there to work.

No one has ever supposed that you can be taught to act and no one who has given the matter much thought would go to an acting school in order to find out. All actors and actresses are, to some extent, 'naturals'. I suppose it has something to do with a prolonged childhood. Which is why children can sometimes give dazzling performances without being taught. I should add, not without a hint of glee, that I have known some children who have been horrible actors. From my point of view the Academy did two things of paramount importance: they taught me to speak, not in a 'RADA' voice, but in a reasonably standard English without the suburban cockney undertones it had before. Clifford Turner and Frederick Ranalow were the helpers here. A great many actors of different generations owe a lot to their skills. The other facility the Academy provided was a shop window. Every performance on the stage of our little theatre would be attended by actors' agents or the representatives of professional managements. How many attended would vary enormously, but for the annual medal awards which were held outide the Academy at a West End theatre, or for the lesser Kendal award which was held at RADA, there would be a big turn-out of talent scouts. You could assume that in the course of two years everyone at RADA was seen at least once by every important agency and management in London. If you had something to sell it would probably be bought. Without implying any criticism of the repertory system (of which I am a firm believer), you could spend ten years in those days in the provinces and not be seen by anyone.

There was no particular method of teaching. Individual teachers had their own ways of going about things. There was no revolutionary 'method' as started by Strasberg in New York. At that time the 'Guide Book' for some of us was the aforementioned Stanislavsky. Hardly a day went by without some reference to him but there was no conscious attempt to put his ideas into practice. His teachings were simply synonymous with truth and absence of 'ham'. It was as uncomplicated as that.

The lessons could be divided into two main channels: the production classes where a teacher (sometimes an actor or actress who was at that time working in the West End) would spend his days producing a class in a full-length play with the parts divided among the members of the class. There was a fair chance that the students would outnumber the parts that the author had in mind so the principal roles were apportioned to different pupils. Apparently on one memorable occasion during the war the audience had to sit through five acts of *Hamlet* with a different Hamlet in each act. They were all girls.

There was a permanent staff who performed the same function, that is, producing the classics and standard repertory plays, maybe taking some three or four weeks over a production. On the whole, because they were more experienced at handling students, their productions had more value. One woman in particular stood head and shoulders above her colleagues: Fabia Drake had been a star in her day: her Rosalind had been finely received. Formidable now in middle age, she dominated the classroom. Some might say that she dominated too much, but Fabia was interested in only one thing: the truth. Any inflection, emotion, gesture or intonation that appeared to her to be other than utterly genuine was ruthlessly exposed. Her eye and ear never relaxed. Her voice, when she came to give judgement, brooked no argument. Usually, in my view, she was right. Her advice was always honest and she in her turn rewarded honesty with compassion. A smile from Fabia was worth a couple of Gold Medals.

In only one area did I find myself at odds with her. I think the majority of actors prefer to read the part over and over again until they have understood it and then, gradually, they will start to learn it, carrying the script and reading from it while they plot their moves and digest the character. This was Fabia's way. My own way is to learn the part as quickly and as well as I can and get rid of the script as soon as possible. Like Garson Kanin and Noël Coward I prefer to know it first and try and work on it and understand it afterwards. We exchanged a few friendly blows over this, Fabia and I. Certainly I have never understood people who 'cannot learn it until they have been given their moves'. It doesn't work in the film studio.

In the main with all the instructors the teaching consisted of giving advice, a little guidance, a hint here, a hint there. Every one of the teaching staff worked according to their own rules.

Zetterling (aged 13) in her 'first real
'—that of a witch. Critics said she
ed 40'—the highest compliment in her
eyes!

Ann Jellicoe in 1960.   (Roger Mayne)

Peter Sallis (centre) with (from left): John Neville, Eileen Barry, unknown, Alan
Nunn in Clive Ryder's production of Ghosts.

Lee Montague (right) with his cousin Lennie.

Paul Bailey.

Hugh Whitemore in 1959.

Anna Calder-Marshall. (Mik

Most of the rules, since they were founded on experience, had a validity of their own. For instance, in the early days I worked out every detail of every minute that I was on the stage. My scripts were inundated with notes that I had given myself. Hardly a word that I spoke did not carry a footnote. I remember one script of *Paola and Francesca*: poor Stephen Phillips, the author, barely got a look in, it was smothered with my own notes on gestures, inflections and emotions. (I was a music snob so there were a lot of 'molto adagios' and 'con brios' and fff's and ppp's.) After the production had ground to a halt while the rest of the cast waited for me to remember my next note the producer, Colin Chandler, gently indicated to me that it might be better next time if I felt more and thought less.

Another producer working there at the time was Ronald Kerr. His experience was largely of repertory and he managed to convey a sense in the rehearsals of what it might be like to work in rep. The production of *Macbeth* which we did with him had two casts. Robert Urquhart quite rightly played the Scottish king in one cast, and I, a rather more unlikely choice, played it in the other. Both productions were done in ten days. At that time to play the role in ten days seemed to me an enormous achievement. Ronnie Kerr dismissed it as being all in the day's work.

Two other names come to mind: Maurice Colbourn, a distinguished Shavian who treated the author with as much respect as he felt he deserved (to sit in on a class with him while he cut Shaw's text of *In Good King Charles' Golden Days* was an experience), and Denys Blakelock. 'Dear old Denys,' I find myself thinking. The course was designed to last two years. Sometimes a pupil would be offered the opportunity to jump a term and, effectively, finish the course in less than two years. This was offered to me but I turned it down. Perhaps I was unsure of myself, perhaps the symmetry of the course appealed to me and I was reluctant to disturb it, perhaps I simply wanted to delay the time when I would be let loose on my own into this highly competitive profession. Whatever my reasons, it was a blessing I turned it down because it gave me the opportunity to work with Denys. A sensitive and skilled actor in high comedy, he produced me in Sheridan's *A Trip to Scarborough* which was a refinement of Vanbrugh's *The Relapse*. I played Lord Foppington, and Denys wittily and constructively guided me through it. The work I did professionally in Restoration and eighteenth-century comedy after leaving the Academy was greatly helped by his advice.

The other area of tuition was what I suppose one might call the 'technical side'. I have mentioned the voice production and diction classes of Messrs Turner and Ranalow. There were, in addition, fencing, movement, dancing, mime and make-up classes. I don't suppose that over the years these have altered all that much, although I hope the generations that came after me didn't get the same advice about make-up. Did our genial, bearded instructor have a vested interest? While we rubbed liberal quantities of 5 and 9 into the palms of our hands, 'Wash your face in it, boys,' he would exhort us.

Fencing, movement and dancing classes I would happily have done without. The movement classes for me had no special purpose; besides which it was clear that we had, most of us, a deformity of some sort or another. Initially we were required (both men and women) to walk around the perimeter of the classroom while our mentor, Theo Constable, pinpointed what we had wrong with us. Almost without exception we had one shoulder higher than the other and most had bent spines. Mine still is, and one shoulder has left the other standing. Corrective exercises were prescribed. I don't know how many were cured. I wasn't, but that was no fault of Theo's. I simply wasn't very interested. The biggest sensation I managed to create in the movement class was sartorial. Clothing, as well as food, was still rationed. Clothing coupons were scarce and the additional casual wear required for moving about with bent spines and unequal shoulders was over and above what I could provide. Even shorts were out of the question. My mother had the answer. Taking the U-shaped tails of two of my old school shirts she joined them together at the sides and stitched an inverted V-like gash in the centre which was supposed to accommodate my crotch. It provided embarrassment, mirth and, on occasion, an almost uninterrupted view of my genitals, giving to basic movement a short-lived and exaggerated notoriety.

Mime was an undemanding exercise watched over by the elegant and quietly spoken Mary Philips, but, in general the 'physical' exercises, dancing, fencing, etc, made little impact on me. It was unlikely that with my personality and physique I was going to make much of a showing in doublet and hose, and time has shown this to be true. John Gielgud in his autobiography has indicated the importance that such exercises and training had for him, but John Gielgud was destined to play princes. I was more likely to be a shop assistant, albeit well dressed.

One of the most colourful personalities among the teaching staff was Hugh Miller. I cannot at this distance of time be sure why Hugh Miller had not made a bigger impact on the theatre than he had. Endowed with a sophisticated mien, a handsome leonine head, a cultured and attractive voice, Hugh brought us a glimpse of the world of Clifford Odets, Noël Coward and the Savage Club. Although he directed many productions at the School, the lessons which I remember best were called 'technique': the technique of acting. 'All you need to know in thirteen lessons.' Hugh enjoyed himself immensely, telling endless stories of the theatre which we lapped up; setting us problems—'Your mother has just won the pools and poisoned your father with weed killer: demonstrate how you open your latest income tax demand while hearing her news and light a cigarette at the same time, bearing in mind that you are left-handed and hard of hearing'—and solving them effortlessly himself.

Later Peter Barkworth took over the mantle of Hugh and distinguished himself by the way he conducted his own 'technique' lessons. Peter was a contemporary of mine, and perhaps some of Hugh's enthusiasm was handed down to him.

I find it difficult to assess how valuable these lessons were. To me technique has been synonymous with experience. The process of opening and closing doors, working with props, conveying the meaning of the author while at the same time performing some additional business has become easier as I've grown older and as I made sure that they were subservient to the main course of action. Today I admire young actors who seem to carry out business without any sense of strain, apparently without effort. Perhaps they have all been taught by Peter Barkworth!

Every generation seems to improve on the previous one. With the exception of the 'greats', the Keans, Irvings, Terrys, Oliviers, Gielguds, I am sure that each succeeding generation, matching and reflecting the taste and spirit of its time, gets better. The average student of acting today is, I suspect, better than his or her equivalent in 1946. The young have no fear of anything today. Or so it seems to me.

The only proviso I would make is this: there was no television worth mentioning immediately after the war, one was trained almost entirely with a view to working in the theatre. Technically the latter is a far harder business. Perhaps today young people do not work for long enough periods in the theatre, by which I mean repertory. Sometimes one can detect weaknesses in young actors who go directly into television and have to sustain large and important parts without the experience that a grounding in repertory brings.

It's fun for me to look over the roll call of those who were there at the same time as I. The women seem not to have survived as well as the men, which is perhaps not surprising when one takes into account marriage and child-bearing and the fact that there are always more parts for men. Leora Dana, an American actress in the Katherine Hepburn mould, impressed us all with her assurance and innate professionalism. Diana Fairfax, Elspeth Gray, Margaret Wolfit, Romany Evans (now in journalism) and Hilda Braid have all gone on to do fine work. Of the men, Robert Shaw, I suppose, has gone the farthest in terms of wealth and fame. But there is a good solid core of theatre and television actors one can see today. Along with those I have already mentioned are Fulton McKay, Brewster Mason, Brian Wilde, the late Nigel Green, Terence Longden, James Gilbert, Alan Sleath and John Neville.

John Neville was clearly destined to be a, if not the, leading romantic actor of his day. The right height, the right looks, a fine, deep-chested voice; he was everybody's—certainly my— idea of a leading man. I remember giving my slightly Roland Culver–ish version of Sir Toby Belch to his Orlando, and I remember playing one of those 'strands', Eng, I think it was, to his Oswald in *Ghosts*. But best of all I remember playing the auctioneer in Galsworthy's play—was it *The Skin Game?*—to John's auctioneer's assistant. *I* had all the words and all the hard work while he went to sleep. Decked up to the nines in whiskers, muffler, mittens and raincoat, he acted me off the stage without saying a word. He nodded off throughout the whole frenetic, nerve-shattering auction. It was then that I knew he was, at heart, a character actor. I suspect he still is.

James Gilbert started as an actor and went on, via the Glasgow Citizens Theatre and other successes, to produce for the BBC's Light Entertainment Group among other things *Last of the Summer Wine*, which landed on my doormat in 1972 and turned into one of the most enjoyable happenings in my professional life.

In 1946 words like chauvinist, homosexual, pragmatic and lesbian were not on everyone's lips. At the age of twenty-five I don't think I had much idea of what a lesbian was. I had a fair idea of what a homosexual was: I'd been one myself for about ten minutes at the age of fourteen. Philip his name was, and I thought he was smashing. The Academy, apparently, was a place where such desires, certainly between chaps, could take root. It hadn't occurred to me but it had occurred to our Principal. I was called to Sir Kenneth's room one day and found that Robert Urquhart and Harold Goodwin had also been summoned. For a time we didn't realize what Sir Kenneth was getting at. We were under no obligation to tell him anything, he insisted; but if we had any suspicion that any male—not female, you'll notice; even Sir Kenneth was unable to bring himself to admit that possibility—had homosexual tendencies, we had only to refer to him obliquely (the chap with web feet and auburn hair in 4B?), and that man would be expelled. There would be no need, he said, to give any reason, he would simply be dismissed.

He then got down to basics. A rubber sheath had been discovered which upon forensic examination was found to have been used upon (if that is the correct preposition) a male. It had been left lying about in the boys' room. I know I was embarrassed. I'm sure Bob and Harold were too. None of us said a word. How frustrating for the old man, who was striving, against his better instincts which told him that sneaking was taboo, to rid his School of any hint of depravity. He clearly felt that his best chance lay in organizing a fifth column, and probably he had chosen us as likely to be three fairly normal males. I don't think we could have answered truthfully even if we had wanted to. I still had an image of a homosexual as a (preferably) young man with one hand chronically embedded in his hip. It never occurred to me that they might enter down left disguised as postmen or policemen. The affair blew over. One or chaps did leave, though with no help from the fifth column. At the time it seemed a not insignificant incident. I have no idea how this kind of thing would be handled today.

The culmination of two years' work was the Public Show, for which a West End theatre was rented for the day. I like to reflect that in my case it was a 'classic' theatre leased at that time to Basil Dean and later to the Oliviers—the St James's. As I have indicated, the public showing meant jobs for those leaving the school. Some jealousy and envy arose out of the casting. It was inevitable that some should have better parts than others. I believe there was a genuine attempt to cast on merit, on the basis of one's work over the two years and, in any event, if there was any unfairness, I imagine it was nothing compared to what one was likely to encounter in the tough theatrical world outside. The Public Shows were well attended by parents and relations, but more particularly by agents, impresarios and talent scouts. I wouldn't like to guess how many of those who took part in the show that I was in were rewarded with jobs as well as medals as a result of it. If I were to say ten per cent it might not sound much, but it is a competitive business and, at that time, I doubt if one person in ten in repertory up and down the country could expect to be signed up to act in or near the West End.

To draw a conclusion and a curtain on my time at RADA I would say that I would gladly do it again. I loved the time that I was there. I didn't find it difficult. I liked the people. I still like them: theatrical people are on the whole interesting, humane and broad-minded. I felt that I was a square peg in a square hole. All my life I have been happy to toe the line. The Academy welcomed line-toers. (There's another word for them, which may explain how I came to win the Principal's medal.) If my son had wanted to be an actor instead of a director I would have been proud if he had gained a place at RADA. I haven't been there since 1948. I have no idea what it is like now, but I can take it on trust. I expect things have got better: they usually do.

Lee Montague

Born in London in 1927, Lee Montague began his theatrical career, after wartime service with the RAF, with a scholarship to the Old Vic School. After two years as a student, he joined the Old Vic Company and during the next two seasons he acted in Twelfth Night *with Peggy Ashcroft, played Edmund in* King Lear, *appeared in* Henry Vth, *in Tyrone Guthrie's productions of* Timon of Athens, *and* Tamburlain the Great, *and in* Bartholomew Fair. *His first American film was John Huston's* Moulin Rouge, *after which he was selected to play the lead in Moss Hart's play* The Climate of Eden *on Broadway. Other films include* Billy Budd, Mahler, *and most recently,* The Legacy. *His West End debut was in* The Matchmaker, *and this was followed by a season at Stratford, highlighted by a role in Peter Brook's production of* Titus Andronicus *with Laurence Olivier and Vivien Leigh, which later toured Europe.*

Lee Montague has played in well over a hundred television plays, and won the TV Actor of the Year Award in 1960. In 1962 he returned to the Old Vic as Shylock in The Merchant of Venice, *Angelo in* Measure for Measure, *and Face in Guthrie's production of* The Alchemist. *Other successes have included* The Latent Heterosexual *at the Aldwych Theatre, a Broadway production of* Entertaining Mr Sloane, Who Saw Him Die? *at the Haymarket Theatre,* The Father *at Stratford East,* What the Butler Saw *and* Skin of our Teeth *at the Royal Exchange, Manchester, and, most recently,* Cause Célèbre *in the West End.*

It was 1948 when I started at the Old Vic Theatre School. The war was not long over and there was a spirit of change in the air. London was full of young men like me, fresh from the forces, eager for a new start. In the theatre there was the same mood—revolution, enthusiasm, new beginnings. Theatres all over the country had been bombed, television was making itself felt, there was a need for a new formula. The Old Vic School was, I think, one of the first places where the seeds of a different sort of drama were sown. Mind you, those days were still well before anyone thought of looking back in anger at the kitchen sink, and if actors were not quite hopping through French windows looking for tennis partners, they certainly had a tendency to sound like gentlemen. I was straight from the East End, via the ranks of the RAF, and had terrible trouble with my vowel sounds. But I'd made it. I'd got to a drama school through grim determination and a series of lucky accidents.

My first piece of luck came when I was about fifteen. I was bored and at a loose end, and my cousin Lennie said, 'If you've got nothing better to do, why don't you come along to the club?' The club was the Brady Boys' Club in the East End and there I discovered Acting. It was a revelation. Every Friday evening after that when I went for my weekly scrub at the Poplar Street Baths I used to come back via the public library and take out piles of plays and books about the theatre. I'd found a whole new world.

The Air Force held things up for a while; somehow the squadron pageant didn't quite measure up to what I had in mind—not that I really knew myself what I wanted. Then came my second piece of luck. I was stationed in London, still doing plays at Brady Street in my free time, but getting restless. Charles Spencer, the manager of the club, said, 'Toynbee Hall is what you need—the drama there is terrific.' It was; it also had Mamie Watson. She was head of drama there, and at the same time happened to be teaching at the newly-opened Old Vic School. For some strange and wonderful reason she took an interest in me and persuaded me to have a go at the audition for the school. Then she set to work on me. Every day after my daily stint sorting out the pay account problems of His Majesty's RAF officers (by then I had reached the exalted rank of corporal), I used to go to her house in Victoria Road in Kensington. There were long windows looking out onto the garden, there was a sitting-room cluttered with books and full of flowers, there was Earl Grey tea and the amazement of being with a woman like Mamie. I'd never met anyone like her before. She was of that breed of English gentlewoman who dresses in tweeds, with wisps of hair forever falling down, a clear and beautiful voice—and a will of steel. She was exuberant, kind and inspirational. I think she did more for me than anyone either before or since. My acting style then was laughable—talk about tearing a passion to tatters! I was so full of passion that my knuckles used to turn white and you couldn't hear a word I said. God knows how she did it, but between us I got a scholarship to the Old Vic School. She'd done more for me than that, though. In her own delicate way, she had formed a new life for me.

I had always lived in Bow, in the East End. My parents were Jewish immigrants, my father a small-time tailor. It was all very poor, very foreign, very remote from anything to do with the theatre. When I got the scholarship, my mother's only reaction was, 'Do you get a living wage?' That was all she had to say. Later on, when she saw me for the first time on the stage, playing of all things a poor Russian student, she said indignantly to me afterwards, 'Couldn't they have given you some decent clothes to wear?' My family didn't disapprove of the career I was embarking on; they just had no idea what it was about. In their world, if you weren't a tailor and turned out to be clever at school, you went in for medicine or the law. I was a mystery; they didn't discourage or encourage me— although when it came to it they did let me use the front room for practising my diction and improvisation exercises. That was quite something. All our family life went on in the kitchen. The front room was kept for storing the Passover wine, for the consuming of the vast quantities of food we put away both before and after the fast on the Day of Atonement, and for when my Uncle Joe came over once every five years from Montreal. I lived at home all the time I was at the Old Vic School. Every day I cycled from Bow to the Waterloo Road and into a different world.

It was a world of Pirandello and Chekov and Shakespeare, of the mysteries of characterization and make-up, of diction classes with a beautiful woman who taught us folk-songs from Mauritius, and of an exotic Viennese dancer teaching us how to move. And for me, above all, a giddy world of lovely untouchable girls. They drove me mad, all those girls with their middle-class accents and rose-petal complexions. The girls I'd known before had been sharp little sparrows from the Hammersmith Palais and the Streatham Locarno, or girls in the WAAF—the highest I'd been up the social scale was a warrant officer. These nymphs from the suburbs were something new to me. All my sexual confidence fell to pieces. Every time I opened my mouth the wrong noises came out. I was horribly aware of my cockney accent, my thick glasses and spiky hair. It did one thing for me though. Hell, I thought— if I can't make the birds, I'm going to be a bloody good actor.

There was every opportunity to be bloody good if you really

wanted to. The school was run by a powerful teaching team:
Glen Byam Shaw, George Devine, and the éminence grise of
the whole outfit, Michel St Denis. He really created the
personality of the school, and gave it its very special style and
direction. He was a man of tremendous personal charm—his
French accent got heavier and heavier the longer he stayed in
England—and terrific drive. He had come over to England in
the 'thirties to direct John Gielgud, George Devine and Harry
Andrews in Obey's *Noah*, and decided to stay. During the war
he broadcast to France and had the distinction of teaching
Churchill how to deliver his speeches. Who knows, without
him 'blood, sweat and tears' might never have been the same.

The idea behind his teaching, and behind all the teaching
at the school, was to live the characters. That is over-simplifying
it of course, but that is basically what it was all about. Like
Stanislavski before him, whom he greatly admired and often
quoted, he wanted to find the truth, the artistic truth. Again
and again he told us, 'Be true to the character, true to the
author; never impose upon the character or the situation what
is not true.' With this idea as our aim, when we first started
working on a play, before any rehearsing, he would get us to
read a scene very quietly—no 'acting', no projection. 'Be an
instrument, not a conductor,' he would say. 'Let the character
find its own way out. Think of a little bird: if you clench your
fist, you kill it; if you hold it too loosely, it flies away. Find the
balance, and you will find the point of control.' After the first
reading, and before we went any further, we would write
character studies. This meant thinking about the whole life
history of the person we were going to play, about his mother
and father, his childhood, his attitude to other people, what he
wore and what he liked to eat. After that, minute analysis of
each line in the play, with painstaking examination of every
nuance of feeling. At this stage, Michel used to tell us, very
occasionally we could get a glimpse, only a glimpse, of the
character we were playing.

The real difference between this approach to acting and any

other was that whereas actors quite often start a characterization with externals—a walk, for instance—we were always
taught to start with the inner life of a character. 'Look inwards,'
we were told, 'think back; *why* does he do it like that?' St Denis
had devised all sorts of exercises to help us do this. We had
classes when about ten of us would have to 'feel' together what
it was like to be in a rowing boat, to feel without looking at
each other the same movement of the rhythm of the water, the
swelling of the tide; or what it was like to be in a coal-mine,
crouching as we edged our way along the tunnel, the horror
as we felt together the rising of the water. He tried to make us
feel aware of the vibrations emanating from other actors, even
when no one was speaking. We had to do individual improvis-
ations as well, and I think it was in one of those classes that I
first got the feeling of being accepted by my classmates. We
each had to mime a trade that day. I chose something I knew
very well. My friend Dave's father was a cobbler; I'd spent
hours as a kid watching Mr Levine at work. So I just did it.
I held the shoe on the last, made a sort of rhythmic movement
with the knives, put the shoe on the polisher and felt it digging
into my stomach as I pushed it forward, and all the time talked
with a mouth full of nails. The class clapped. I was a success.
    I wasn't quite such a success when it came to working with
masks. This was another exercise to get us to let a character
break through the confines of our own bodies. We had to put
on a tragic or a comic mask, and wait for something to take
over without forcing it in any way. If it worked, it was sens-
ational. I saw one guy in a comic mask being transformed; his
whole body seemed to change and gradually take on the mood
of the mask. I used to put on a mask and wait hopefully;
nothing ever happened. Which is funny when you think of my
animal study, and how I saw myself. This was another St
Denis special. He sent us all to the zoo: 'You must train your
eye and learn to observe everything. Choose an animal with
whom you feel sympathy, then come back to me and improvise
—let me see the animal take over.' What, for some weird

reason, did I have to choose?—a chameleon. Now, chameleons don't do very much apart from camouflaging themselves. So I just stayed very still giving off essence of chameleon. I stayed very still for about ten minutes, occasionally flicking out my tongue. St. Denis watched me intently. Finally he said, 'That was good, very good. But boring.'

He was always very grudging with praise. There was a terrible happening three times a year known as the end-of-term 'verbals'. Teachers and pupils gathered together in one room, and one by one we each did our stuff, to be publicly criticized and assessed. The day of reckoning. There was a sort of awful excitement about it. Up until the end of my second year I'd been grateful if St Denis had proffered a restrained, 'Not bad, not bad at all.' Then one momentous day it happened. I had been working all that term on a scene from *The Seagull*. At the end of my last speech he said slowly, 'Let me put it this way; your performance of Konstantin—that was acting.' That was the turning point for me. I was in ecstasy, six feet above the ground—and committed for good and all.

Glen Byam Shaw—another great man, another great influence. Ruddy-faced, suave, darling of the West End theatregoers, and yet a man of infinite patience, even love, for his pupils. He more than anyone gave me an idea of the mystery of acting. 'Evenings are the time for magic,' he used to say—he always liked working late into the evenings. He was a marvellous teacher. We were supposed to work on one play a term, but he worked with such concentration and in such detail that we were lucky if we did one scene in those ten weeks. He would never hurry anything. He always had time to take us individually into a corner during rehearsal and chat about the part we were playing. When something we were doing actually began to work, he had the ability to show us the excitement of that breakthrough. He would feel with us, even cry with us. Complete involvement was what he demanded. To him the theatre was a sort of church. He allowed no chatter, no knitting or newspapers in a rehearsal room. If you were not part of the act of worship which was a rehearsal, then he told you to get out. I remember once seeing him, after a rehearsal, sweeping the stage at the Old Vic with what was almost a caress—it was an altar to him. Acting was his passion. If you were receptive—and God knows I was—there was no limit to what you could learn from him about the theatre.

John Blatchley was altogether different, but no less an influence. He was a lot younger than the rest of the staff; not so experienced as a teacher, but closer to us. He bridged the gap for us between mystery and practicality. He had been an actor—and a very good one, too—and came from a family of real old troupers. They had all been in music-hall, and lived a life of travelling from one provincial theatre to another, a life of tatty boarding-houses and Sunday trains. John used to tell a marvellous story about the time he was on one of these slow, dirty old trains with his Mum and Dad, and loving it— train journeys were the only time they had together. His parents were so determined to keep the carriage and their precious privacy to themselves, that they stuck winkle shells (they had eaten the contents for their Saturday tea) all over young John's face. Anyone who popped their head into that invitingly half-empty carriage got a very nasty shock indeed and departed pretty sharply. I suppose that what John taught us more than anything was how to live as an actor, how to survive this grinding profession. He showed us, for instance, when to stop. How to know when one has done enough work and to know the moment to relax. In the middle of a highly-charged performance once, emotion quivering in the air, he suddenly stopped dead and started to muck about, showing us how to play some daft football game with pennies. He was always full of humour and good sense. I was lucky enough to spend my first two years as a professional actor with him. Many were the 'digs'—dreary theatrical boarding-houses— which were cheered by his company—such as the place we shared in Liverpool with Leo McKern and Douglas Wilmer. There we all stuck very closely together, since if any one of us appeared alone, especially on the stairs at night during a visit to the lavatory, we were in danger of immediate sexual assault by the lady of the house. John taught me how to enjoy life—one of the most important lessons I reckon I ever had.

All the classes we had at the school, and all the teachers, were part of the same thing—cogs in the machine. The aim was to break us down. That sounds a bit sinister, but all it meant was to try to make us completely receptive. Some people were too rigid ever to become malleable enough to get there. Our voices and bodies had to become instruments, reflections of the roles we were playing. One of the methods was the physical approach, getting rid of our body tensions from head to toes. This was one of my greatest problems. I always seemed to end up with my shoulders under my ears. Any emotion—and up came my shoulders; by the time I got to page eight I was exhausted.

Litz Pisk was the lady in charge of loosening the knots. She was a dancer from Vienna, mysteriously ageless and yet seeming to us to have always been old. Her grey hair was pulled back into a tight bun, she always wore a black high-necked jersey and skirt, and she was as lithe and supple as a cat. She didn't seem to have any bones in her body. She had immense energy, and was a warm and forgiving creature. She needed to be with me; what with my tensions and my short thighs I found her classes a bit of a struggle. We would start every day with three-quarters of an hour of bar exercises, then go on to do the dance of different periods—a good way, this, of getting us to feel history through our bodies, to forget our modern selves. When we danced a pavane she made us imagine the stateliness of the costume, the stiff, pointed style—I loved that puritanical mood, the cold Gothic quality. I never came to grips with Restoration stuff and all those minuets, but came into my own with Victorian jollity and the Lancers. The movements of history, the movements of emotion; she taught us to express feelings in the way we moved, to make our bodies take a different shape, even to feel what it was like to be a tree reaching far into the sky.

From Litz we dragged our stretched limbs to Suria Magito, a straight-backed, full-bosomed Russian lady with black hair and the carriage of a queen who taught improvisation classes, then on to the Hungarian Jani Strasser who taught us voice production. Real barnstorming stuff this; how to project our voices, how to make them resonant, and above all, how to *breathe*. Jani had a touch of the Richard Taubers and seemed to have stepped out of a Ruritanian extravaganza, except that he lived in West Hampstead. He was all dash and style, dapper and lavender-scented, with a deep voice, a monocle, and always with a flowing handkerchief and four inches of cuff showing.

When it came to actual diction, we were taught by the enchanting Geraldine Alford. She was that old-fashioned thing, an elocution teacher. She was patient and caring, and very desirable. All of us men were a little in love with her. She was slight and elegant, with innocent eyes and beautiful skin and an incredibly mobile mouth. 'Use the tip of the tongue, it's the most active part, the main organ of articulation—say, "Two toads totally tired trotting to Tewkesbury".' And we, lascivious and fascinated by her darting tongue, would say, 'Do it again for us, Geraldine.' We all looked forward to the odd quarter of an hour when she would give us individual coaching. I was in the enviable position of needing more extra help than anyone. She had virtually to do a Henry Higgins transformation on me, and I enjoyed every minute of it. My Bow Road accent must have been quite a challenge to her. I was the classic cockney, with the dropped final g's, the glottal stop, the sibilant t's, the deformed diphthongs and never an initial aspirate. I spent hours in front of the mirror watching my lip formation when I said OO, OH, AW, and studying my jaw and tongue position for my AH, AY, EE. As I struggled to say 'tea' instead of 'tsea' I pored over Geraldine's notes and her crisp instruction, 'The articulation of tongue tip with tooth ridge should be firm, clean and light with no unnecessary escape of breath,' and solemnly repeated, 'You won't make top nor tail of it, Tom, till you've heard it two or three times.' Where did Geraldine find them all? 'The suitability of a suet pudding without superfluous plums is a superstition presumably due to Susan's true economy.' Not to mention that folk-song from Mauritius we all intoned together which started with the stirring lines, 'Ca-ri-la le milah-tress, Tow pick soo-soo na.'

All the tongue-twisters and the interminable repetitions of 'Peeminy—Payminy, Beeminy—Bayminy' were working towards one goal only: to make us easy to listen to. It was not a 'BBC' nor an 'Oxford' accent Geraldine was teaching us. I don't know, maybe at other drama schools students were still learning how to speak like gents, but times were changing and the image of an actor was becoming less of a stereotype. At the Old Vic School all they wanted to do was iron us out a bit. A regional accent is inhibiting; my East End accent could come in handy sometimes, but I had to learn to become 'accent-less'. Only in that way could my voice be a flexible instrument for getting across a character. It was all very much part of the Old Vic philosophy; the voice, like the body, must be free—free to express a great range of emotions. Any tenseness, any irregularity of speech created a barrier between you and your audience.

Back at Antill Road in Bow, I shut myself in the front room and worked and dreamed. Every night I would come home from the school to the turbulent life of the East End. There was always a good smell of cooking, eternal arguing, and a lot of worry. From my bedroom at night I could hear the thump of the fourteen pound iron as my father carried on with the pressing. He got paid for each suit he made and pressed, so he worked late and long. I used to earn the odd pennies when I was a kid by taking out the basting cotton from the jackets for him. He led a hard life, but had his fun too—the only words of English he could ever read were those connected with horses, the jockeys and owners and trainers, but I always had to write out his betting slips. As he got older he got down to making one jacket a week, but it kept him going. When he couldn't lift the iron any more, he gave up and died. My mother was always the dominant one at home. She was proud and strong, cherishing her husband and seven children, keeping the house gleaming and clean in the face of the East End soot and grime, and turning every meal into a banquet. Any spare time she had was spent basting seams, felling armholes and sewing on buttons for my father.

I used to give my mother most of the £1 10s grant I got from the LCC every week, but began to find out there were things I needed money for—contact lenses, for instance. I always took my glasses off on stage—they didn't look too hot with doublet and hose—and as a result, every time anyone threw me anything, like a coin or a sword, I missed it. My friend Dave and I decided to have a stall in the market at Roman Road in Bow. We sold anything we could get our hands on, mostly rather weary cosmetics since Dave's brother dealt in those in a Hounsditch shop and we could lift stuff when our stocks were getting a bit low. Every Saturday we did it, flogging rain-spotted bottles of 4711 by the light of the hissing naphtha lamps strung above the barrow. At Christmas we went in for toys for the kids, and for a while did a brisk trade in sheets and tablecloths. Dave was articled to a solicitor, but had a poetic line in market patter. 'Look at this, Madam,' he would holler, waving aloft an embroidered cloth, 'kippers on this would taste like caviare.'

It wasn't only the need for money that made me want to work in my spare time. I found it more and more difficult to reconcile the excitement of the school with my humdrum existence at home. I was leading a double life. I was ashamed to bring anyone back to Antill Road, and ashamed of feeling that way. I couldn't see that it was that very atmosphere, the mixture of being Slavic and Jewish and poor and emotional, that made me need to be an actor and to express my feelings of being an outsider to the world. But then, in my raw and insecure state, I needed to keep my two worlds apart. I had to get through the vacations somehow, so one summer I went with a gang of other Old Vic students to work at the Malvern Festival. It was the first year the festival had been revived after the war, and we were employed as stage hands. We must have been unbearable. That year they were putting on two plays by Shaw and a couple of modern plays which we thought were too trivial for words. There were the real pros like Francis Day, Ernest 'Thesiger, Dermot Walsh and Denholm Elliott giving it their all while we swanned around sniggering at the old hat scenery—I remember having to crouch behind some flats depicting rocks which we had to rush at in the half-dark and change into sand-dunes—and spending a great deal of time hanging about in the wings talking loudly about Stanislavski. The reaction of the cast was unfriendly: 'For Chrissake stop talking and move the f – – – – – scenery!'

It wasn't only at Malvern that we were accused of arrogance. We did tend to think of ourselves as a sort of élite, and the reaction of the rest of the theatrical world was that we knew all about Shakespeare, but when it came to the reality of playing in rep—the true working theatre of rehearsing and performing a play in a week with the express purpose of giving entertainment—we couldn't cope. Maybe they were right. Certainly the methods we were taught, with the deep analysis of character and all that bit, only worked with plays which were in themselves deep—and good. 'We're just no good at rubbish,' was the lordly attitude we adopted.

Elitist or not, the atmosphere of the school was quite unique. For one thing, a lot of our time was spent in the Old Vic itself; from the very beginning we lived and breathed the real live theatre. We rehearsed on the stage of the theatre, had history of drama lectures in the dress-circle bar, learnt about make-up in the dressing-rooms, discussed stage management in the corridors. After two years in the school we were allowed to become apprentices to the company. Very humble stuff, but intoxicating to us. We understudied the understudies, and played all that host of Shakespearean walk-ons from Roman soldiers to Illyrian citizens. I remember once getting a fan letter for my sensitive performance as the bear in *The Merry Wives of Windsor*.

The fourth year we were fully fledged and became members of the Old Vic Company, a company which after all included Alec Clunes, Roger Livesey, Paul Rogers, and Peggy Ashcroft— I'll never forget how beautiful she was as Viola in *Twelfth Night*; she knocked me sideways. They were marvellous to us raw recruits, those distinguished actors and actresses. Just watching them work was magic, and we learnt so much. As we stood to attention as soldiers and canopy-bearers behind them, we learnt that important theatrical lesson: how to stand still on stage. While we watched we saw how the professional actor behaves, how to deal with emergencies; for instance, how to react to unexpected laughter from the audience, like the famous moment when the public were rolling in the aisles at the lines from *Henry V*, 'Ay, but these English are shrewdly out of beef!'—that was 1950 and the meat ration that week had gone down to one and tuppence worth. I remember watching Leo McKern putting on a body make-up when he was playing an old man; painstakingly and with infinite care, by applying highlights and shadows, he aged his muscles. I thought ruefully of my own efforts which until then had been geared to speed rather than artistry; the spray gun which made me brown in blotches and remarkably like a jigsaw puzzle; the permanganate of potash which was a smashing colour but made me itch; and the never-to-be forgotten photograph of myself as libation-bearer to Catherine Lacey's Clytemnestra—arms held high, dark brown all over, with bright white armpits.

But what we learnt more than anything from acting with the company, green as we were, was love. Love of the theatre, of its traditions, and the eternal excitement of being part of it. In October 1950 the Old Vic theatre re-opened after the war. The first production was *Twelfth Night* and we students were to be graceless but eager Illyrians. The dress rehearsal went on until four in the morning, and when we finally emerged, exhausted, we saw that the queue for the first night was already stretching out of sight round the theatre. That night, before the curtain went up, Edith Evans came out and spoke in that unforgettable voice of hers the lines, 'London be glad, your Shakespeare's home again. . . .'; we knew once and for all the real meaning of being an actor.

There had never been a drama school quite like it in this country, with its complete marriage of teaching and performing. Tragically it only lasted for five years but in that short time its influence on the theatre in Great Britain was enormous. A lot of my contemporaries have become important actors—Alan Dobie, Keith Michell, Joan Plowright and Derek Godfrey are just a few—but it was far more than a school for actors. It produced designers, technicians and directors, and out of it came Frank Dunlop who ran the Young Vic, Caspar Wrede and James Maxwell of the Royal Exchange, Manchester, and Chris Morahan of the National Theatre. Glen Byam Shaw and John Blatchley are now directors of opera at the London Coliseum. John runs the London Drama Centre as well. Norman Ayrton was co-principal of LAMDA; George Hall is in charge at the Central School. What we were taught, and the methods used to teach us, have spread throughout the English theatre scene.

I know that the influence of the school on me is immeasurable. The total commitment of all the teachers there made us totally committed. I still am now. I still approach a role in the way I was taught. To this day when I get a new part I sit down and analyze the character the way I did with Michel St Denis. I still need an hour on my own before I go on stage to get myself into a part, and I think I still act 'from the inside'. There is no right or wrong way to learn how to be an actor, of course; the Old Vic just happened to suit me.

My final launching into the outside world came from the school, too, from my mentor Glen Byam Shaw. I'd been approached by Moss Hart, the king of Broadway, to play the juvenile lead in the New York production of *The Climate of Eden*. I felt pretty grand, sitting at a meeting in a private room at the Savoy Hotel with Hart and Byam Shaw, but I was in an agony of indecision. Should I leave the familiarity of the Old Vic theatre, where I could cosily embark on another season, for the cold unknown of Broadway? Glen Byam Shaw looked at me, quizzical and wise, and said, 'The theatre, you know, is not an insurance policy.' I knew what he meant, and he was right of course. In this profession there's no knowing if you'll ever be asked twice, so you learn to take your chances as they come.

I accepted the part on Broadway, and left for New York soon after that. I think it was only then that my mother realized what was happening to me. America was her Mecca. If she'd had the extra five pounds when she left Lithuania she would have gone on to the States where the streets were paved with gold; she hadn't, so she stayed in England. When a Rolls Royce arrived at the house to take me to the plane for America, she knew her boy had arrived. That was when she decided at last to open the front room, invite all the friends and relations, and have a party like she'd never had before. I wasn't there, of course. But then I'd left Antill Road in more ways than one.

Paul Bailey

In December 1950, at the age of thirteen, I made a decision that was to change the whole course of my life. 'I am going to be an actor,' I told my disbelieving mother and amused friends. What I didn't tell them was that I was going to be a *great* actor—another Gielgud, at the very least. That was my huge ambition.

I had recently taken the leading role in the school play. As Sarah, Duchess of Marlborough, in Norman Ginsbury's *Viceroy Sarah*, I performed like one possessed. I stormed; I screamed; I shed real tears. In costume and make-up—a woman of the world—I was radiant. On stage, I forgot the ever-present drabness of my South London home; the view (and smell) of the gas works that greeted me each morning. I told Queen Anne what was good for her; I treated the wily Abigail Hill with a proper suspicion—my involvement with Sarah was total. Assuming her character, I knew the power of artifice. For three memorable nights, I said goodbye to my dull self and became a forceful personality, a creature of violent contrasts. I had never known such happiness.

A long, dismal year passed before I acted again. The following December, I appeared as Emma Woodhouse in a trite adaptation of Jane Austen's great novel. No storms, no tantrums: I was calm now, and not a little smug, and not a little bitchy. But I was deeply ashamed when reminded of my rudeness to Miss Bates, and touched and honoured by Knight-ley's declaration of love: mine was a complete absorption. For three cold winter nights I lived in the eternal summer of that marvellous work—Emma's best speeches had all been lifted straight from the book. I was strengthened in my resolution to adorn the theatre one day. Soon after, I started to learn *Hamlet*—the play, not the part—by way of preparation.

For I loved Shakespeare. I'd seen *Twelfth Night* and *Henry V* at the Old Vic, and had been entranced. I remember walking back to Battersea from the Waterloo Road, declaiming the immortal lines along the Thames Embankment. I saw John Gielgud as Leontes and knew that I had to emulate him. Hearing him say 'O, she's warm!' in the final scene of *The Winter's Tale* was one of the magical moments of my boyhood. I saw his Benedick, too, and was dazzled—nothing less—by the deliciously arrogant way in which he manipulated the audience. A raised hand was enough to stop their laughter: 'You thought that was funny,' he seemed to be thinking, 'but wait till you hear this.' In time, I would learn to play comedy with that casual perfection—so I assured myself on those days when I wasn't planning my first Macbeth, my definitive Cassius.

In December 1952 I appeared as a man at last. I wore a long robe instead of a dress, and I sported a beard. I was Henry IV, the unhappy father of Prince Hal. I'd wanted to be Hotspur, but the producer insisted that only I could give the king his due. I felt cheated, and I sulked. I found Henry an awful old bore to begin with: he just sat on his throne and moaned, and sitting on a throne and moaning didn't require much in the way of acting, I thought. I was wrong, I soon discovered. Act Three, Scene Two of *King Henry IV, Part I* tests the actor playing Henry to his limits:

> 'I know not whether God will have it so,
> For some displeasing service I have done,
> That, in his secret doom, out of my blood

He'll breed revengement and a scourge for me;
But thou dost in thy passages of life
Make me believe that thou art only mark'd
For the hot vengeance and the rod of heaven
To punish my mistreadings . . .'

It is a wonderful scene: it gives us the measure of the true
Bolingbroke, the state of 'sun-like majesty' he aspired to and
attained. It is a scene full of sorrow and anger. For three
nights, I was angry and sorrowful with my profligate son on the
school stage, and when the scene was over I stood in the wings
and listened to the applause I considered mine by right.

An actor and producer named Jordan Lawrence saw me as
Henry and told me what I wanted to hear: that I should think
seriously about the possibility of becoming a professional actor.
He advised me to audition for a place in a good drama school,
and he offered me a job in a Christmas show which would
shortly be opening at the Leatherhead Theatre. I met the
producer of *Buckie's Bears*—an entertainment devised by the
pseudonymous Dr Marie Stopes and her young son sometime
in the 1930s—who assured me that I was the ideal person to
take on the taxing roles of Gnome and Baby Bear. And so, for
the vast sum of £2 a week, I made my first appearance on the
professional stage at the ripe age of fifteen. Instead of speaking
Shakespearean verse, I was singing:

'O, Buckie's bears in the zoo one day
Locked up the keeper and ran away
And no one knew but me and you
And nobody saw them leave the zoo . . .'

I wish those lines would run away, but they won't. Their toe-
curling awfulness apart, they remind of a happy time—I was
among real actors, sharing a real dressing room (in which, one
dreadful night, I made the mistake of quoting from the
Scottish play, and was chastised accordingly), listening to the

wonderfully frivolous theatrical gossip of real troupers. Returning to school that January, I was desolate.

Early in 1953, I auditioned for a place at the Central School
of Speech and Drama and, to my amazement, was accepted.
Shortly after, I repeated my audition (Richard II's final
soliloquy) before a forbidding board representing the London
County Council. I was awarded a scholarship—my school fees,
plus £60 a year on which to live. I was well and truly on the
road to greatness.

In those days, the Central School was situated high up in the
Albert Hall—I can't recall which floor, but it sometimes felt
like the ninetieth: the long climb reaching it certainly kept one
in trim. So cocky and arrogant at my grammar school, I was
suddenly afflicted with shyness and a debilitating lack of
confidence when I entered the attic, as it were, of Albert's more
useful memorial. I became aware, as if for the first time, of my
origins: I was a working-class boy among (mainly) upper- and
middle-class men and women. (When one is sixteen, nineteen
and twenty-year-olds seem very grown up.) The girls were
especially forbidding: to some of them, the Central was a
finishing, rather than a drama, school. They took their holidays
in Paris, or Venice, or somewhere in Barcelona. I was acutely
conscious of my clothes: you could see your face in my shoes,
but they weren't made of the best Italian leather. At the end
of my first term, I was asked by an ex-debutante what I was
giving my mother for Christmas. I replied that I would find a
present costing about £2 or £3. Her laughter was derisive; I
was accused of being a Scrooge. I was too ashamed then to tell
her that the home in which I lived had no bathroom, and that
I had to brave the elements whenever I needed to go to the
lavatory. (We plebs became the new snobs in the '60s, when
no one who was anyone came from a stately pile or a suburban
villa.)

There were worse problems. With my new-found lack of

confidence came an awareness of my physique—or lack of one, to be accurate. I resented being thin. I wanted to creep into the woodwork—an ambition I came near to fulfilling. I hated the movement classes I was forced to endure every day. Why, I wondered, did the hour for exercise pass at a slower rate than the one for voice training? I felt everyone's eyes on me. I was gawky and graceless, and it showed.

I was in a hurry to act, and acting meant Shakespeare. For weeks on end, we had to keep our mouths shut, for the course began with lessons in mime. Having to remember exactly where I opened the door or drew the curtains was a task that often had me screaming internally. Damn the door, sod the curtains. No Marcel Marceau, I didn't do too badly, however. Two of my silent playlets come to mind: in the first, I was trapped in a lift, with hysterical results; in the second, I was a driver examining the body of someone I had just killed. I was a morbid youth.

One memorable day, a girl of the finishing school persuasion performed—or rather, failed to perform—the most ineffectual mime imaginable. Nothing stayed in its proper place. She went through the whole pointless enterprise with complete indifference. She finished. She turned and looked at the teacher, waiting for his verdict. It came, after a lengthy pause: 'And balls to you, too, dear. Next!'

The teacher's name was Oliver Reynolds. Oliver was, and is, a man of few words—all of them considered; all of them apt. When he spoke in class, it was always to convey something of a practical nature. He didn't waste time theorizing. If one was giving a good performance, he encouraged one to do even better, but shoddy work he instantly and firmly disparaged. He kept us on our mettle: we *had* to give of our best. His disapproval, like his praise, was honestly felt and as honestly stated. He made us think for ourselves. When directing a play, he persuaded us of the importance of working as a company, however small—and seemingly unimportant—the parts: a maid with one line to say was there for a purpose. He did this without mentioning Stanislavsky, or indulging in heady talk about acting as an art. His means were simple and direct, the product of much hard thought. In his presence, working well was a duty and a necessity—gabbling on about Art was not the way to get a production on stage. We did a lot of gabbling in our three years at the Central School, but never when Oliver was around.

In my second term, I played Mercutio—in one scene. I can't recall if I was good, bad, or indifferent. I do remember that I was terrible as one of those yokels at the beginning of *Romeo and Juliet*, and that some months later Restoration comedy turned out *not* to be my forte. In Middleton's *Women Beware Women*, I indulged in the Voice Beautiful (a vice I was prone to when speaking poetry, and for which I was constantly reprimanded by the voice teacher, Cicely Berry) because I hadn't a clue how to play the character, whose name has temporarily gone from my memory. In a lacklustre piece to do with Theseus and the Minotaur, written by Patric Dickinson in immediately forgettable verse, I was brilliant, though. (That's what everyone said, and I'm taking them at their word.) The part was a true challenge: an old man reflecting on past events, sadly and wearily. I revelled in his sadness, and I think I got inside his skin.

I played other ancients in my teens: Captain Shotover, in Shaw's *Heartbreak House*, was the best of them. His wisdom/ lunacy appealed to me. In my final year, as wise Professor Paulet in Priestley's *People at Sea* (Priestley at his priestliest; a cautionary tale with Life as its subject), I sank without trace. Shaw's nautical philosopher, even at his most bizarre, seemed to be composed of flesh and blood, while Priestley's pipe-smoking, profundity-prone Prof was the merest cardboard. I lacked the skill required to make him believable. In Rattigan's *Who is Sylvia?* I was slightly younger—my performance as a colonel in late middle age embarrassed me as much as it must have done the audience. I had a single scene, a comic one, in which I was supposed to be blind drunk. The laughter from the auditorium was noticeable by its absence.

I saw myself as a juvenile lead, but no one shared that vision with me. In play after play I was a 'character' of one kind or another—usually some dodderer whose presence in the next world was eagerly awaited. Why was it always me? After all, So-and-so looked much older, and Such-and-such's pronounced stoop was constantly commented upon, while You-know-who had *real* grey hairs—if only around the temples. Yet *they* played the handsome young lovers, the charming cads, the witty sprinklers of *bon mots*. My seventeenth year was spent in heavy disguise. While others used Leichner to enliven their youthfulness, I picked out the duller colours from my make-up box. Anaemia, thy name was Bailey.

A house in Hyde Park Gate, long since demolished, which the school rented, was a more attractive setting for lessons than the Albert Hall. One hot afternoon, a group of us read *Uncle Vanya* there, under the guidance of a teacher who kept referring —for a reason that was hers alone—to *Mister* Chekhov. 'What do you suppose Mr Chekhov meant by this?' she would interrupt. Never plain Chekhov, or Doctor Chekhov—that perplexing 'Mister' resounded in our ears. Mr Chekhov, we learned, was a master of pathos. I read Astrov, I remember, in Act Two. As a result, I spent several happy months reading everything Mr Chekhov wrote: plays, stories, letters. I have re-read them all, with renewed admiration, many times since.

That same teacher, with more justification, also referred to *Mister* Maugham—the author, few will remember, of a play called *The Breadwinner*. I executed, in more senses than one, the title role. At least I didn't look anaemic—my cheeks wore a boozer's flush. 'Savour that wonderful language,' Teacher advised. 'Mister Maugham is a master.' Master he may have been, but not—I decided—on the day he committed that drab little comedy to paper. I waddled about on the Central School stage, desperately trying to convey the brazen cocksureness of a not very confident middle-aged man. My desperation showed. Walter Hudd, who adjudicated the production, found my performance embarrassing. So did I.

In the final year of the Central School course our regular acting teachers abandoned us. Professional producers came and put us through our paces. Shakespeare was behind us now. Apart from an Ibsen play—*The Pillars of Society*, in which I appeared briefly as a local dignitary named Krapp—most of the plays we rehearsed, and eventually showed to the public, were staple West End junk. This, we were rightly told, would be the type of stuff the majority of us would be acting in once we were in the profession. I still shudder when I think—and I try not to—of a play by the then unDamed Agatha Christie called *The Hollow*. I was mercifully murdered at the end of the first act. A shot was fired off-stage, I clutched my chest, I muttered 'The South of France . . . The smell of mimosa . . .', staggered down a flight of stairs, and expired. Raymond Westwell, who directed this less than thrilling piece, made me fall down those bloody stairs at practically every rehearsal. The relief after executing that fall for the last time was immense. 'The South of France . . . The smell of mimosa . . .': what else would one say when one had just been fatally wounded?

In that final year, we were all told to prepare audition speeches. Each one of us was to perform for about three minutes. We were to choose something that showed off our particular gifts. After all, a large part of our early years in the theatre would be spent auditioning, rather than acting. A distinguished actress would present an award to the boy or girl 'who gave the most touching performance'.

I wrote my own speech, which I pretended was a translation from the French. The French theatre was very popular in the '50s—at least with the posh critics. Sunday after Sunday le Chevalier Hobson went into ecstasies (and French) over Madame Feuillère's triumph in some 'masterpiece' by Claudel or Giraudoux. My playwright's name was André Bisset. His masterpiece had the sonorous title *Les Deux Figures de Jésus Christ*. I let my close friend, Pat Keen, in on the secret. No one else knew that Monsieur Bisset was a product of my imagination.

Bisset's anti-hero had necrophiliac tendencies. In one start-

ling scene, he confesses to a shocked priest that he has—er—
done something—er—unmentionable—with a young—er—
female. The scene closes with Gérard revealing that he had
murdered the young female first. The combination of Bisset
and Bailey had a stunning *effet* on the audience. When I got
up from the confessional position and shuffled off, you could
hear the silence. Prolonged applause followed.

The distinguished actress was stunned, too. She was also
shocked that such a talented young actor had chosen such
a—er—distasteful scene from Monsieur Bisset's play. Why
hadn't I chosen one of the other scenes? André Bisset, she went
on to say (to my scarcely controlled delight) was undoubtedly
a major dramatist. She couldn't recall the titles of his other
plays off-hand (*surprise, surprise*) but he held a high position in
the French theatre. I looked at Pat Keen, who was wearing a
devilish grin. I smiled. If the distinguished actress should read
this article, I can now inform her that Bisset's other great work
is entitled *Chez Myrtle*. It is mentioned on page 109 of my novel
Peter Smart's Confessions.

My happiest memory of those Central School days is of
Beatrice Lillie. Oliver Reynolds told me to go and see her show
An Evening With Beatrice Lillie at the Globe Theatre. I went. I
went again. Accompanied by Pat Keen, I went again and
again to hear Bay-ah-tree-chay, the mezzanine soprano, render
'There are fairies at the bottom of our garden':

> 'You wouldn't think they'd *dare*
> To go merry-making *there*,
> But they *do*! Yes, they *do*!'

and to see and hear her revengeful maid impersonate the
mistress of the stately home: 'We went on safri last year
[pronounced 'yah'] to Africa, you know.' This observation
prompted a question about how many animals were bagged.
Beatrice Lillie obliged with a list which included 'leopahds'
and 'tigahs'. This prompted a further question: 'Did you have

a bison?' 'Goodness, no, we used a bucket.'

I loved Beatrice Lillie's exquisitely controlled lunacy; her apparent unawareness that an audience was watching her; her total lack of sentimentality. Other students were amazed at my fondness for her: they found her cold, and her artistry too private to be funny. Yet her art has made an abiding impression on me: its sublime irrelevance is something I cherish. Should I ever be abandoned on a desert island, a projector, a screen, and a copy of her silent film *Exit Smiling* would ensure my continual spiritual well-being and sanity. Buster Keaton is her only equal.

In June 1956 I and my fellow students appeared in a special matinee performance at Her Majesty's Theatre. There were excerpts from three or four plays. I was a dotty mountaineer in Denis Cannan's *Misery Me!* The *Times* reviewer found me funny: I had a gift for comedy, in his opinion. School was over now. My acting career had begun.

Twenty-one years later, I find myself in the small city of Fargo, North Dakota, recalling the origins of my scarcely illustrious contribution to the English theatre. After drama school, what was there for me? Well, there were those suicide-inducing theatrical lodgings, ruled over by vindictive land-ladies. I can laugh at them now, but they came close to scarring my spirit then. There was Nurse Birdsey's abode in Coventry. Nursie, a religious fanatic, gave her two young lodgers one fried egg for breakfast. Not one egg *each*—no, one fried egg, sliced in half, between us. 'Why do my eggs always break?' she would ask sweetly, pretending there were two of them on the table. Nursie kept a walnut wardrobe in the dining-room: inside, under a pile of knickers of the passion-killer variety, she hid the tin of drinking choclate from which she extracted a teaspoonful apiece for her 'boys' on cold winter nights. And there were other places, other ladies. The one-eyed landlady with a 'past', and her ancient dog whose loud farts accompanied our every meal: 'Patsy's dreaming', she would say, pointing to the recumbent beast. Oh yes, there were countless others.

What plays did I appear in? *The Prisoner of Zenda*, for one. The leading 'heavy' had a lisp: ' 'Tis her bwother, wed-headed Wudolf of Wuwitania,' he announced in the opening scene. There was a play whose title I've forgotten, but from which a solitary line occasionally comes to haunt me: 'You realize, of course, that this is blackmail?' One night, the actor playing the blackmail victim got drunk and a new line emerged: 'You realize, of course, that this is Blackpool?' There was *The Teahouse of the August Moon*—I was the Goat Boy, my bare feet covered in goat shit whenever I left the stage. There were thrillers; there were light comedies. I am still, I tell myself, sane.

But there were, thank God, other plays. The one I remember with most affection was Ann Jellicoe's *The Sport of My Mad Mother*. I played Cone in its first production at the Royal Court Theatre. Kenneth Tynan wrote that my performance 'especially needed pruning'. At least he noticed me. I played in Shakespeare, too. Loosely. A cough here, a spit there. As Lovel, in *Richard III* at Stratford, I surpassed myself one evening. I dried. I couldn't remember the two lines:

> 'Here is the head of that ignoble traitor,
> The dangerous and unsuspected Hastings.'

Christopher Plummer, playing Richard, waited and waited for me to speak. Then he pointed at the head I was holding and inquired:

> 'Is that the head of that ignoble traitor,
> The dangerous and unsuspected Hastings?'

To which Lovel, nodding vigorously, replied 'Yes.'

The year I spent at Stratford was the gloomiest and the most absurd of my entire life. I returned to London, anxious to leave the theatre but not knowing what other job I could possibly do. I'd begun to dislike the vanity and ridiculousness of actors; the specious 'brilliance' of directors intent on improving Shakespeare's plays. The fact that the posh critics lavished praise on the latter only made it worse. Years afterwards, in my novel *Peter Smart's Confessions*, I was able to put the absurdities of that time in some perspective.

Where did my training for the stage lead me after Stratford? It led me to Harrods, the store of stores, where I saw life in the raw. Only the English upper class knows how to make an insult sound like a compliment. A mere shop assistant now, I received many such compliments. I listened a lot behind those counters. I would stop sometimes and think 'What have I done with myself? Did I study at the Central School for *this*?' And then I'd remember that one of my English masters at the grammar school had once said that instead of going into the theatre, I should have tried for a place at Cambridge. And then I would feel a sense of waste.

Yet I lingered on in the business until I was twenty-seven. I was in several television plays. My last big engagement was in a television series built around Shakespeare's Roman plays, *The Spread of the Eagle*. One critic wrote that I was 'the worst Soothsayer in living memory'. What a notice to go out on! *E finita la commedia*.

I am glad now that I went to the Central School, and not to a university. I am among academics here in the great Midwest, and I like appreciating them at a distance. My years in the theatre were my training-ground as a novelist. I was well away from Literature (which I read voraciously, of course, in grisly provincial dressing-rooms and flea-ridden boarding-houses) and that was good for me. I met all kinds of different people; I saw something of that everyday lunacy Dickens celebrated with such awesome energy; I looked and listened.

I can now see, with the advantage of hindsight, that some part of my brain was telling me, as early as 1955, that I would be a novelist one day. The invention of André Bisset had something to do with it. In the summer of that year I worked as an invoice clerk for the publishers, Chatto and Windus, and was radiantly happy—I was still at an age when the people in books were more real to me than live human beings. During that summer I read all Turgenev's novels. When the supply ran out, I felt a sense of deprivation. In the autumn, I returned to school—to raincoated police inspectors; wise old professors; mimosa-smelling victims; to the study of an art I was to abandon before I was thirty. Actually, it abandoned *me*. It said to me, loudly and clearly, in a hot and stuffy television studio, 'Stop. Think what you're doing.' I stopped, and thought. I had caused it enough worry. I walked out of the Television Centre in West London, having made another momentous decision.

Hugh Whitemore

Hugh Whitemore was born in 1936, studied at the Royal Academy of Dramatic Art, acted in provincial repertory theatres, and then worked as a publicity writer for Associated-Rediffusion until his first television play was produced in 1963. Since then he has written for all major BBC and ITV drama programmes, including The Wednesday Play, Armchair Theatre, Play of the Month, Elizabeth R, Theatre 625, *and* Play for Today. *With many original plays to his credit, Hugh Whitemore has also written over 20 adaptations, winning Writers' Guild Awards for his dramatizations of* Cider With Rosie *and* Breeze Anstey (*which was seen in Granada's* Country Matters *series). Many of his television plays have been seen throughout the world, and in America his work has been screened in* Masterpiece Theatre *and* The Hallmark Hall of Fame. *He has also written extensively for the cinema, his most recent screenplay being for the film version (starring Glenda Jackson) of his own play,* Stevie, *which had a smash-hit run at the Vaudeville Theatre in 1977.*

Hugh Whitemore is married to literary agent Sheila Lemon, and they have a young son called Tom.

Looking back, I find it difficult to understand why I was so eager, so determined to go to drama school. My family background was resolutely untheatrical (I had seen no more than a dozen plays during childhood and adolescence), my experience of acting was limited to a tremulous appearance as Alonso in a school production of *The Tempest*, and my voice was a poor instrument: I had an unfortunate tendency to speak much too fast, to gabble and trip over my words. Nevertheless, I was hopelessly stage-struck. I spent hours mounting elaborate productions in a home-made model theatre (fantasizing a dazzling career as a director/designer), and wrote several very long plays in various styles ranging from Rattigan through Christopher Fry to John Whiting at his most symbolic. But it was as an actor that my day-dreams reached their grandiose peak, and I firmly believed that I possessed a huge, undeveloped talent that would soon be recognized and acclaimed.

Much to my parents' distress, I abandoned the idea of going to Cambridge and wrote to the Bristol Old Vic School, asking for an audition. I performed one of Big Daddy's speeches from *Cat on a Hot Tin Roof*, drawling all those Deep South vowels and strutting around the room in what I hoped was an appropriately raddled manner. There cannot have been many times when this role has been attempted by a spindly English schoolboy, and I suspect that my reckless nerve was more impressive than my talent. But I passed the audition and my confidence grew. If I was going to spend two years studying the theatre, wouldn't it be better, I thought, wouldn't it be more exciting to spend those two years in London rather than Bristol? I wrote immediately to the Royal Academy of Dramatic Art.

By return of post I received a list of audition pieces, and with very little hesitation chose the shortest: Hamlet's misanthropic speech from Act II, Scene 2, which includes the famous passage beginning 'What a piece of work is man! How noble in reason! how infinite in faculties! in form and moving, how express and admirable' and ending with that sour question, 'And yet, to me, what is this quintessence of dust?' Although I had seen the Olivier film, *Hamlet* was not a play I knew well, and I found the prospect of studying the entire work extremely daunting. The speech seemed to be straightforward enough, and I decided that it was most probably a light-hearted, albeit jaundiced, commentary on the human condition and would best be delivered with crisp sardonic humour. I prepared it in the swooping, exaggerated style of Frankie Howerd, who was then my favourite comedian. Thus I performed it, one hot summer's afternoon on the small stage of RADA's rehearsal theatre. I created a tremendous impression. The adjudicators were full of praise for my originality, and told me that of course I would be given a place at the Academy. Furthermore, they suggested that I would be wise to come back the following week to try for a scholarship. My fellow-auditioners were stunned when I boasted of my success; they had been told that all candidates would be informed of the results by letter. Clearly I must be an exceptional exception to have broken such a rule. And so I arrived for my first term with some sort of a reputation flying before me. It took no more than three weeks for everyone to realize that the adjudicators had been guilty of a rash misjudgement.

It was cold and raining when I travelled up to London for the beginning of term. My heart was heavy with grief. This was not one of those much-looked-forward-to day-trips, this was something very different. I would not be returning. I was leaving home for good. As the train clattered towards Waterloo, I looked out at the lights along the Embankment and knew with a total certainty that my life was, at that very moment, undergoing a profound and irreversible change. A rare experience.

During my two years at RADA I lived in a succession of rented rooms and shared flats. For a time, three of us occupied the attic of a hotel near Baker Street. The other guests were lonely, Rattigan-like old ladies, one of whom took a great interest in me and frequently invited me to her room to share her smoked-eel sandwiches. We had a slot-machine television set in our room, which was a great luxury, and our favourite programme was the Goons' 'A Show called Fred'. One evening, the announcer broke into the programme with the news that British troops had invaded Suez. We hooted with laughter, convinced that this was just another manifestation of Goonish humour. One of my attic partners was a handsome and relatively well-off American, who enjoyed an unusually varied and active love-life. In order to get our bedroom to himself (and his latest girl), I would be bribed with five shillings to spend the evening in the Baker Street Classic, followed by a cheese roll and coffee in the Moo-Cow Milk Bar.

On one such evening, having sat through *Fallen Idol* for the second time in a week, I returned to the hotel and was irritated to find that the bedroom door was still locked. I rattled the handle and heard subdued scuffling within; I went to the bathroom and sat, fully clothed, in the empty bath until I heard my American friend and his girl creaking down the stairs. I gazed wearily at the disordered bedroom, and climbed into my pyjamas. Suddenly, the door flew open and the hotel manager confronted me in high rage. 'I'll thank you to leave my maids alone, you sex-mad bastard!' he screamed. Shortly afterwards, I moved to Brixton.

I shared this new flat with Christopher Greatorex, who, like me, soon abandoned acting for another career: he now runs a notable restaurant in the Oxfordshire village of Chesterton.

Even in his student days Christopher was an excellent and ambitious cook, and, as far as our limited means would allow, we lived in some style. The flat itself was fairly comfortable, although it did have one very odd feature: the bathroom was part of the landlady's kitchen, and only a plastic curtain separated the two halves of the room. Thus, when one stood up in the bath one's head and shoulders rose up above the top of the curtain. It was a curious experience, rising to wash the genitalia, to be confronted by the landlady sipping tea.

The Royal Academy of Dramatic Art was housed in a tall, thin building in Gower Street. Inside was a maze of stairs, corridors and classrooms, with two theatres: a small rehearsal theatre deep in the basement and the larger, grander Vanbrugh Theatre, where the senior pupils gave public performances. The entrance hall was dominated by a large, multi-coloured timetable, nicknamed Rainbow Corner. I write about it in the past tense because it seems to me to belong to the past, to another life almost. I can scarcely remember the day-to-day routine; like my ambition to act, the memories have faded, and I can no longer associate myself of the 'seventies with my alter ego, that young drama student of the late 'fifties.

The most striking member of the staff was the voice production teacher, Clifford Turner. He was a tall, elegant man, who looked more like a diplomat than an actor. He always wore a dark blue suit, a sober tie and shirts with a monogram on the breast, which I thought was the height of sophistication. He had a boomingly resonant voice, and seemed to regard his pupils with an amused, benevolent contempt. We would sit in a semicircle around his chair, chanting vowel sounds and fiendish tongue-twisters.

> 'There was a young fellow named Carr
> Who took the three-three for Forfar,
> For he said, "I believe
> It will probably leave
> Far before the four-four for Forfar." '

Movement and ballet classes were conducted by Madame Fedro, a formidably attractive woman who had once been a leading dancer with the Ballets Joos. Dressed in black sweater and slacks, she would lunge at us with pantherish agility, yelling instructions above the piano accompaniment in her vibrant middle-European voice: 'Higher, Louise, raise ze arms higher!' She found my Christian name quite impossible. 'Huth!' she would cry, as I tried to hide at the back of the class, 'lift your zighs, Huth!' But my thighs were unused to being lifted and I found Madame Fedro's classes something of a torment, redeemed only by her pianist, a splendid musician called William Blezard. With unkempt hair and eyes glittering behind thick spectacles, he would coax cascades of the most wonderful music from RADA's battered upright.

We were also taught how to use stage make-up, how to fence and how to mime being a tree. We were advised to polish the soles of our shoes so that audiences should not be offended if we were to cross our legs on stage. We were given hints on Audition Technique by Denys Blakelock, a gentle, literate, sad-eyed man who had been a prominent actor in the 'thirties; Brian Wilde taught me to do the tango for a production of *Ring Round the Moon*; and a fierce lady called Mary Duff frightened me so much that I was incapable of doing more than the train effects for our end-of-term show, *Random Harvest*. What we were not taught were the unpalatable truths of the theatre: that most of us would not be able to earn a living on the stage, that many of us would struggle on until it was too late to attempt another career, and that all of us would suffer a succession of humiliating and sometimes crushing disappointments.

The most important and influential lesson in my theatrical education took place not at the Academy, but at the Royal Court Theatre. Until the mid-'fifties, my play-going had been restricted to Shakespeare and West End comedies, both of which I enjoyed and both of which were totally removed from my own personal experience. Thus, I seldom thought of the theatre as having anything to do with life as I knew and lived it; it was a medium of adult make-believe and poetic fancy. Suddenly, literally overnight, my attitudes were changed. When I saw *Look Back in Anger* I saw people I recognized; people who thought as I thought, people who said things I wished I was clever enough to say. A group of us became Osborne fanatics. We knew the play by heart, and would drop appropriate lines into the conversation whenever possible. 'The Platitude from Outer Space' became our common term of abuse, we teased our girl-friends about their noisy behaviour saying that 'even a simple visit to the lavatory sounded like a medieval siege', and to this day I cannot hear Vaughan Williams without thinking 'something strong, something simple, something English'. Osborne changed my view of the theatre, and since I have always worked within the theatrical profession, he changed my life. For me, no other dramatist can command the same emotional loyalty.

As the terms came and went, our varying degrees of ability and talent became increasingly apparent. Exceptional pupils were promoted to the Vanbrugh stage (Siân Phillips's progress was meteoric, I remember), while some of us were kept down, spending term after term in the lower levels as we struggled to master the basic techniques of stagecraft. But no matter how undistinguished our journey through the Academy may have been, we all dreamt of fame. We would sit in cafés (Olivelli's, Bunjies, or the Act I Scene 1) and talk loudly of theatrical matters, glancing every so often at the neighbouring tables to see if anyone was gazing at us with envy. When starry visitors came to address us we would linger in Rainbow Corner, hoping to brush against Jean-Louis Barrault or to receive a smile from Edith Evans. And then, as the seniors left, there would be much excitement as news of them filtered down to us: Jack Hedley was doing a play at the St James's, Tim Seely had got the lead in *Tea and Sympathy*, Peter O'Toole was going to the Bristol Old Vic. But they were the lucky exceptions. Only two of the students who started with me achieved the sort of fame we all then ached for: Susannah York and Brian Epstein, the Beatles' Svengali.

Susannah was clearly destined for stardom from the very beginning, but Brian's astonishing fame in the early 'sixties took everyone by surprise. He and I were classmates during our first term and quickly became friends, sharing as we did the painful realization that our acting abilities were extremely meagre. We would often share a meal in a small café in St Giles High Street (now buried under Centre Point), and then go to see the latest avant garde play at the Arts Theatre. Perhaps as we sat watching Ionesco, the Beatles were strumming their first guitars some two hundred miles away. Brian left RADA after one term, and I scarcely saw him again. I would have liked our friendship to continue, but so dazzling was his éclat during the high summer of Beatlemania that I was shy of making contact with him. I saw him last in a theatre, a few months before he died. Although surrounded by trendy acolytes, we managed to have a few words, mostly about RADA and the humiliations we had shared there. 'Give me a ring,' he said. But I never did.

Although it is only twenty years since I was a student, our attitudes and behaviour seem almost pre-war in their modesty (or was it repression?). The 'fifties were the days of suspender-belts and coffee-bars, the days when youthful male passions were inflamed by a picture of naked breasts in *London Opinion*. Frank Sinatra was singing songs for swingin' lovers, *High Society* was the film we all flocked to see, and young men lusted after Kim Novak in *Bus Stop* and Joan Collins in almost anything. I was, of course, enthralled by the many beautiful girls who were my fellow students, but I never entertained any real hope of seducing them. There were rumours of erotic evenings in an American's flat in Park West, but most of us never experienced anything more decadent than bottle parties and heavy petting in Kilburn or Earl's Court.

Being novitiate actresses, some of the girls attempted a Sally Bowles-ish sexual bravura (*I am a Camera* was still a recent memory), but green fingernails could not disguise their unshakably Home Counties morality. I remember going to the cinema with a particularly attractive (and I thought available) girl who said, as we settled into the back row of the upper circle, 'I think I should warn you that I don't like French kisses.' Although saddened to realize that we were unlikely to advance beyond rudimentary cuddling, I was at the same time encouraged and thrilled that she had envisaged the possibility of more adventurous intimacies.

Homosexuality was suppressed, or at least kept carefully hidden. There were very few effeminate men at the Academy, far fewer than I expected. Changing attitudes are always well expressed by slang; in those days homosexuals were 'queer' and not 'gay'. We had a fresh, almost naive, innocence in the 'fifties, an innocence that now seems immeasurably distant. The passage of time has taken its toll. Two of my contemporaries have committed suicide, and another was murdered by homosexual thugs on Hungerford Bridge.

I can see now that my two years at RADA marked the end of an era. The theatre was undergoing a fundamental change, and I sensed, although at the time I could not put this feeling into words or coherent thought, that the Academy was not keeping pace with this change, with this revolution. We were still instructed as if the theatre meant the West End theatre. Style and technique were hammered into us; intellectual stimulus was ignored. There was an unspoken assumption that audiences left their brains with their umbrellas at the cloakroom, and no one tried to come to grips with the new and challenging movements that were manifesting themselves in Sloane Square and on the Continent. Most members of the teaching staff exhibited a fastidious reluctance to treat acting as a job; we were told how Restoration fops took snuff, but not how to cope with the exhausting routine of weekly rep. Nobody taught us how to talk to an agent, how to make a few pounds as a television extra, how to sign on for the dole. In other words, nobody taught us how to survive. They showed us how to spread the icing, but not how to mix the cake.

Perhaps the realities of theatrical life were deliberately ignored by most of the teachers because they themselves still faced a daily struggle for survival. With the exception of young working actors like Peter Barkworth, Brian Wilde and Joan Newell, the staff was composed of men and women who either had not made the grade or who were in professional decline; they had all the necessary physical attributes (well-modulated voices, telling gestures, graceful movement), but few flashes of creative insight. Plenty of style, but little content.

The heavy hand of class-consciousness was also much in evidence. Regional accents were frowned upon, and every effort was made to 'iron them out'. There were very few working-class boys and girls amongst my contemporaries, and those who had managed to squeeze into the Academy were not encouraged to develop the virtues and strengths that their family background had given them. On the other hand, there was an abundance of upper-middle class girls with minimal theatrical flair, who seemed to regard RADA as a rather amusing finishing school. Nevertheless, interesting talents did emerge, and I remember with pleasure student performances by Charles Kay, Joanna Dunham, Anna Quayle and Peter Blythe.

But there were other good performances, some of them outstanding, by students whose careers never got started or just faded away. What happened to them, I wonder? Most of the girls, I suppose, have got married, and are now leading comfortable lives as wives and mothers; the men, if they have been lucky, might have found agreeable jobs in radio, television or theatrical administration. Some will have given up the theatre completely; others will still be hanging on, waiting doggedly for the telephone to ring, sending their photographs and curriculum vitae to young television directors (who, in all probability, will cast them straight into the wastepaper basket), and wondering anxiously whether the rent will go up next quarter. Of course nobody *forces* them to stay in the theatre, but their courage cannot be denied.

I remember, some years ago, an actor I had known at the Academy was cast in a television play I had written. Our acquaintanceship as students had been slight; he was 'one of the seniors', acting leading roles in the Vanbrugh, and I regarded him with some awe. He was also a very skilful actor, with an enviable technique and self-confidence. But his career had not prospered, and in my play he had the small part of a Bank Manager. Circumstances had conspired to prevent us from meeting during rehearsals and the first time I actually set eyes upon him was in the control gallery, during the recording of the play. His performance did not please the director.

'We'll have to try another take,' he said to the floor manager. 'Tell that sodding Bank Manager to give it a bit of life. He looks more wooden than the scenery.' After three attempts the director turned to me apologetically. 'Well, that's the best we can do,' he said, 'that bugger's more like a puppet than an actor.'

Later, in the BBC bar, the actor and I had a drink. 'That went rather well, I thought, didn't you?' he said cheerfully, and without waiting for a reply began telling me about the various jobs he felt 'pretty confident' of getting during the next few months. A year or two later I saw him playing a butler in a costume-drama serial, but recently he seems to have disappeared from the television screen. But no doubt he is still 'pretty confident' about the future.

My six terms at RADA slipped past (rather like two years spent in a time capsule) without my making much progress as an actor. However, despite the discouraging tone of my teachers' reports, I began to feel myself gradually drawn into the fabric of theatrical life, albeit as a privileged spectator with his toes barely touching the threshold. There were, of course, many cheerful diversions. My friends and I derived much pleasure from being 'known' in the coffee-bar of the Arts Theatre, which was then *the* meeting place for out-of-work actors. We learned how to make one cup of coffee last a full hour-and-a-half and conversed with real professionals, who talked casually about 'my agent', of 'doing a spit and a cough on "Ward 10",' and would tell first-hand stories about Larry or Johnny G.

Some, though, had darker reasons for loitering in the Arts. On one occasion, a very young and virginal girl student (slowly sipping her coffee) was approached by a man who said that he was an amateur escapologist looking for an actress with whom to develop an 'exciting theatrical act'. Innocently, the girl went with him to his flat where she was shown an alarming array of chains, whips and padlocks. She obeyed instructions and bound the man tightly, but as soon as it became clear that his intentions were sexual rather than theatrical, she fled, leaving him handcuffed and chained in the basement flat. We spent much time speculating on his eventual fate.

Every so often, although not as often as we would have wished, free theatre tickets were distributed amongst the students. As a rule, these were for plays that were staggering along on their last legs, and as a result we became connoisseurs of theatrical failure. On one rare exception to this rule, we were told that a few tickets were available for the European première of a major Hollywood film that was being held at the Empire that evening. Lots were drawn, and I won a ticket. What is more, I learned that the adjoining ticket had been won by a girl whose lustrous eyes and sulky lips had fuelled many of my erotic fantasies. I could hardly believe my luck. Being a realist even then, I had never asked this girl for a date, being convinced that she would turn me down. (Not only was she very beautiful, she also came from a well-known theatrical family, and was therefore one of RADA's élite).

I rushed back to Brixton, bathed, washed my hair, shaved, and climbed into my dinner-jacket. I arrived early at the cinema, and strolled across the foyer with studied nonchalance. The Girl of my Dreams glided in, looking staggeringly glamorous. I stared at her, dumbstruck. She stared at me, and quickly suggested that we go straight to our seats. As we walked up to the Circle I glanced at my reflection in one of the ornate wall-mirrors. A tremor of despair scampered down my spine; I looked like a relief trombonist in some cheap dance band. The dinner-jacket was creased and baggy, the bow-tie hung loosely to one side, and the soft collar of my white shirt had sprung up to my chin, where a shaving wound had spotted it with drops of blood. I prayed for the lights to dim, and spent most of the evening wondering how I could cope with the après-film predicament. Not surprisingly, the Dream Girl took refuge in the prior engagement excuse, and I was able to hurry home to hide my shame. I told Christopher, my flat-mate, that the evening had been a glittering success, and hinted that the Dream Girl had permitted a degree of dalliance in the taxi home.

Although I was happy enough to pass most of my days in a fools' paradise, not bothering to think about the future, there were moments when I wondered fearfully what would happen when I left the Academy. I had a certain flair for comedy, but this was offset by poor diction; I had a good grasp of character, but lack of technique prevented me from putting ideas into practice; I knew a lot about new plays and contemporary writers, but that would not help me in finding a job. Nobody seemed to think that I had an outstanding talent for anything, and Peter Barkworth, the most perceptive of our teachers, opined that I might probably find a niche in the theatre, but not as an actor. I tried writing again, and entered the Academy's one-act play competition, only to be beaten by Susannah York.

As the weeks sped past, my search for something to excel in grew increasingly desperate. With a friend who could play the piano, I devised and rehearsed a cabaret act: smart, sophisticated songs for smart, sophisticated audiences. We thought our material was tremendously witty (the lyrics were properly spiced with references to Binkie and Noël), and it was with some confidence that we applied to various night clubs for an audition. One of the first people to reply to our letter was

Clement Freud, who was then running a club over the Royal Court Theatre. We arrived there at midday, with hoovers droning amongst the red plush. Clement Freud told us that it was our function to take people's minds off their steak and peas, and warned us not to use any words ending in -unt, -uck or -ugger. This one audition, an experience of bowel loosening embarrassment, was enough to convince us that cabaret was not our métier. We retired to the pub next door, and drank heavily until closing time.

I left RADA in the summer of 1958. My last performance was in a student production of *Look Back in Anger* (Susannah York was Alison; I played her father, Colonel Redfern). Several of my companions had already got jobs, some of them had even got agents. I departed without being awarded a diploma; my only prospect of making any money was temporary work at Euston Station, selling newspapers. I packed my bags and went home to Southampton, where I lied bravely to my parents and friends, telling them that all sorts of exciting possibilities lay ahead.

I have never returned to RADA. The images that remain with me are curiously disjointed, like time-jumps in an experimental film: the subfusc green of the corridors (but were they green?), laughter in the common-room, the sweaty smell of fencing masks, the thick gravy poured over rissoles in the top-floor canteen, Robin Ray enthusing about Klemperer's Beethoven, all-night parties in a white-painted flat above the Haymarket Theatre, John Fernald's spotted bow-ties, the fencing master crossly demonstrating a move ('Don't look at me, you might learn something'), sprinting up stone stairs in ballet tights, proudly buying sticks of Leichner from a chemist's in Leicester Square, learning lines on the tube to Goodge Street, passionate embraces on the windswept Embankment, weekly visits to the Everyman Cinema, browsing for hours in David Archer's Greek Street bookshop, rehearsing on the flat roof in the summer sun. The memories I have of RADA are, without exception, happy ones; and yet, curiously, I kept no

tangible souvenirs of my time there, no photographs, no programmes, not one single memento. It is as if I knew even then
that my ambitions to be an actor were best locked away in the
past, forgotten and unregretted.

One final memory takes me back to the last few weeks of my
time at the Academy. A group of us went to see a play called
The Party at what was then the New Theatre. It was the play
in which Albert Finney made his London début. Some of my
friends knew Finney, who had left RADA in a blaze of glory
just as I arrived. We all went backstage afterwards, and
my companions crowded into Finney's dressing room with the
usual fanfares of 'Darling!' and 'How marvellous!' For some
reason I waited outside, lingering in the drab corridor and
feeling uneasily that I should not be there. Suddenly, Charles
Laughton, who was the star of the play, came lumbering along
towards me. He nodded a greeting and asked if I was looking
for someone. Hastily I explained that my friends were talking
to Mr Finney, adding, as if to excuse my presence backstage,
that I was a drama student.

'Where are you studying?' he asked.

'RADA,' I said.

Laughton grinned. 'Oh, I went there too.' And off he went
to his dressing room.

I felt unaccountably elated by this brief encounter; Laughton's friendly manner suggested that our shared experience of
RADA created some sort of a bond between us. I felt, briefly,
that he was part of my world and I was part of his. If nothing
else, I thought to myself, I have made a start.

Anna Calder-Marshall

Anna Calder-Marshall was born in London, the elder daughter of the author Arthur Calder-Marshall. She trained at LAMDA for three years, where she was awarded the Ellen Terry Scholarship, and after leaving played leading parts in three television productions before joining Birmingham Rep in 1967. As a result of her performance in St. Joan, *she was offered Ophelia opposite Tom Courtney's Hamlet at the Edinburgh Festival. In December 1968 she appeared in three half-hour plays for NCB/ATV in which she co-starred with Sean Connery, Michael Caine and Paul Scofield. For her performance in this trilogy she won an Emmy Award.*

Miss Calder-Marshall has since played leading parts in several major television drama productions. In 1970 she had a tremendous personal success as Sonya in Uncle Vanya *at the Royal Court Theatre, and then played Cathy in the film of* Wuthering Heights. *Other successes include Cleopatra opposite John Gielgud's Caesar in* Caesar and Cleopatra *at Chichester in 1971,* Absurd Person Singular *at the Comedy Theatre, and a recent tour of England and the Continent with Birmingham Rep in* Measure for Measure *and* The Devil is an Ass.

She is married to the actor, David Burke.

When I was ten I remember hearing Noël Coward sing 'Don't put your daughter on the stage, Mrs Worthington!' I rushed over to the radio to switch it off just in case my mother heard it and took his advice. I needn't have worried. My mother loved the theatre—indeed she outdid my love sometimes.

Once she took me up to London to buy two wigs, as my sister Clare and I were always acting plays for her and my father and any luckless grown-up who might stray in. We got into the train at Waterloo, clutching two boxes containing a splendid white Prince Charming wig and a hideous brown Ugly Sister wig with a bun on the top and cascading ringlets. 'Let's wear them back home!' said my mother. 'Oh I couldn't,' I protested. 'If you wanted to be an actress you would,' she replied. So I did. I asked her if she would mind wearing the white one. I thought that everyone would guess it was a wig, while secretly I hoped that my brown one might just be passable. So we sat, side by side, attracting curious glances. I was having quiet hysterics—but trying desperately hard to keep a straight face, as I did so want to be an actress. Inwardly relieved when we arrived at Twickenham Station, I wanted to take my wig off. 'Keep it on!' said my mother. 'We'll walk all the way down the platform with them!' When we reached the barrier the ticket collector beamed at us and said, 'Had a good time at the Ball?' My mother said she had.

I was terribly impressed by this incident. I thought she was splendid. Both she and my father encouraged the fantasy world that we liked to live in. When Clare and I entered each year for the Horsham Verse and Drama Festivals, they would sit at the end of the sitting-room every weekend while we recited poems and rehearsed scenes over and over again, offering criticism and encouragement. Clare and I both loved acting, but as our strict convent upbringing gave little outlet for it except for these drama festivals, we had to let off steam at home. We often rehearsed at the end of our garden which ran down to the Thames. I remember doing Viola's speech from *Twelfth Night*. On at least two occasions I got so carried away that the rings, which I had borrowed from my mother, fell into the river.

Jean and Beattie de Leon, who still run their drama school in Kew, gave me individual tuition for auditions. Beattie is a small, splendid dynamo of energy. She would greet me with 'Oh good egg!' and we would launch into hour-long sessions.

In the glorious year of 1964 I was accepted by the London Academy of Music and Dramatic Art. I should remember Beatlemania, Carnaby Street and mini skirts, but I don't. I just remember I was in seventh heaven. It was like going back into a fantasy world—and yet this was called training! I was a little young, only seventeen. They usually accepted only students over the age of twenty-one, but I think that they realized it was no good telling me to go to university and then come back.

Once accepted, I was advised by Norman Ayrton (the Deputy Principal at LAMDA) to apply for the Ellen Terry Scholarship. I decided to do the ring scene from *Twelfth Night* and the trial scene from Shaw's *Saint Joan*. I wasn't told who was to judge the auditions, and I planned to meet my parents, who were just as nervous as I was, outside the theatre, or somewhere in the Earls Court Road afterwards. I'll never forget the shock when I asked who the adjudicators were, and was told

Dame Sybil Thorndike, Sir John Gielgud and Fabia Drake. I had heard Dame Sybil on the radio the previous week talking about *Saint Joan* and how Shaw himself had directed her and told her that the speeches were orchestrated like music. She had said that she could remember the inflexions he gave her to that day, and she didn't like hearing other actresses playing the part. I'm not absolutely sure she said the latter, but if she didn't I felt sure she would have done. I was terrified to meet them, but as soon as I was introduced to Fabia Drake and Dame Sybil, who was bursting with life, I relaxed immediately. Sir John was late, and bounded towards Dame Sybil, calling her 'Darling Sybil'—and I thought, They do say it—'*Darling*'. I plunged in, did both pieces, and talked to them afterwards. They were warm and kind. Just as I was leaving, Norman Ayrton told me I had won the scholarship.

I was in ecstasy, and tore out of the theatre. My mother and father weren't outside, so I rushed down the Earls Court Road darting into odd shops in case they were there. Suddenly I saw my father's face looking anxiously out of an antique shop. I charged in to find my mother pretending to buy two glasses. I was crying with happiness and the words rushed out, 'Sir John! Tears in his eyes! Dame Sybil! *Lovely!* I've got it! I've got it!' The antique dealer looked at my mother in astonishment, as if she was responsible for this lunatic child, and both parents backed out of the shop as though displeased with the glassware. We all hugged each other and jumped in the air like silly sheep.

My first impression of LAMDA was terribly influenced by the numerous accounts I had read by Stanislavsky and others, of young Russians attending classes and preparing their parts. It was like watching myself in a dream I'd had. Since the age of thirteen I had devoured every book on acting I could lay my hands on. I subjected my sister Clare to acting exercises at the convent, and once hit her on the head with a volume of Shakespeare's tragedies when she lost interest. And suddenly there I was, in the LAMDA Theatre, a young actress listening to the Principal, Michael MacOwan, talking about Stanislavsky and our year's programme. He was a superb lecturer. He always sat on a table, one leg curled under him, the other touching the ground: he looked like a stork.

Norman Ayrton became Principal of LAMDA in my second year. I owe a great deal to both men, who had great faith in me. I can never thank them enough.

I do remember that in my first term I was thought of as slightly sick in the head by my fellow students, because in my first improvisation I'd eaten somebody, and in my second had chopped somebody else up in a train and thrown the bits out of the window.

I also felt ridiculously young and at the same time hugely mysterious, covering my chubby face with white make-up so as to look like Eleanora Duse. A few students had been to university and were extremely intelligent. If we had debates they just held forth. I thought: how can they think of all these things? How do they come out of their mouths? One student never said a word. We all thought he was very deep and mature and that's why he never spoke. I found out later that he was the same age as myself and had successfully pretended to be twenty-four in order to get in. He was always given mature roles, much to the envy of students who were in fact older than he was. Nobody guessed his secret.

What I found bewildering was being asked to present emotions I'd never felt in situations I'd never experienced. For example, I remember Vivian Matelon (a marvellous teacher and director) saying to us, 'You come into a room, find a letter, open it, discover your mother is dead. You smell something, realize there's a fire, your house is burning down and then you speak, break down, what you will.' I did the exercise and just stood there. After a pause he asked me why I was silent. 'I'm stunned,' I said. I was overpowered by the events he had described. I had no idea how I would react. I just thought, 'How dreadful!' Yet an older actress, Annabelle Leventon, did the same exercise, then burst into a wonderfully moving speech. She must have been to university, I thought.

My year was known as a very promising one. It was exciting. We had a reputation even before we'd put on a production. We were a mixed bag of northerners, cockneys, upper class, intellectuals and artists. Some felt too old to be taught, others that their personalities were being broken down and not built up again. But in the main I think our group had great spirit and were very happy.

LAMDA spelt personal freedom to me. I lived in digs off the Earls Court Road, and for the first time in my life I was alone. I relished it, regarding my small cooker as a king might look at his crown. I lived on yoghourt, frankfurters and kidney-bean stew. My parents had asked a sweet Irish caretaker to keep an eye on me. One night, as I was going through some breathing exercises—starting very quietly, building up to strange grunts and cries and then rounding it off with screams—I heard a desperate knocking at the door. 'Anna, are you all right? Are you ill?' 'I'm fine,' I said through the keyhole. 'You sound so dreadful. Let me come in, my dear!' asked the worried caretaker. She opened the door to find me alone. I wasn't being raped or trying to kill myself. She hugged me in relief. From then on I had to go to new pastures to rehearse.

My room had a beautiful big window overlooking a disused carpark, an ideal rehearsing place. When we did the play, *See How They Run*, I played Miss Skillon, a rather butch middle-aged woman who falls for the vicar and gets terribly tight and starts singing hymns in a way God would not have approved of. We were always being told that we should be as big and expansive as possible, and as my room had proved embarrassingly unsuitable, one evening I stole down to the carpark. It was about ten o'clock, and I practised reeling and tottering as I sang, 'We plough the fields and scatter the good seed on the land', in the deepest tones I could muster and in as pissed-sounding a way as possible. I felt wonderfully free, until I saw lights suddenly switched on in a big house overlooking the carpark and people's heads sticking out of the window. Other lights went on. I slunk away like a guilty cat discovered eating the Sunday joint, and then ran for all I was worth back to my room. But I shall always look back on Miss Skillon with relish. She gave me the chance to wear my first false nose. It fell off in a performance somewhere in the sofa—and I quickly made a new nose in the interval. My mother congratulated me on its change of colour in the drunk scene which followed, ascribing this to my powers of acting, not realizing it was a different nose. I was told off for sitting with my legs wide apart and showing a pair of long woollen bloomers, but I said, 'Miss Skillon would do that! It's the whole point. She's not aware that it is wrong.'

Derek Goldby (the director) backed me up. He was a great stickler for authenticity. When we did *Live like Pigs* by John Arden, we had great difficulty in making the gipsy characters disgusting to the actors playing the middle-class parts. Their reactions weren't real. I was playing the youngest gipsy, and as an experiment Derek told me to go and roll in the mud outside the rehearsal room. It was winter and conveniently very muddy. I obediently went and covered my face and hands with dirt and returned to Derek. 'That's not enough,' he said. 'Go back!' So I returned to the challenging mud and literally rolled in it. I was soaked to the skin and squelched back to the rehearsal room. 'Oh go away! You're filthy!' cried my fellow actors, who had just arrived for rehearsal. 'That's your gut reaction. Remember it!' said Derek.

The following Sunday, inspired by his direction, I dirtied my face, and wearing a filthy old mac, took a tube to the East End and tried to track down some children who resembled my character in the play. I was taking it very seriously, feeling a bit schizophrenic—half of me dressed for the part, the other half aware I was behaving like a sleuth, pressing my back against walls, peering round corners. My make-believe world was shattered when two grubby kids pointed at me and said jeeringly, 'Look at 'er! Ain't she funny! Wot does she think she's doin'?' I walked away. I felt cheated of my role as an invisible observer.

The most frightening moment I had at drama school was when I totally identified with a part. We had a very exciting American group led by Stacy Keach, who believed in groups intermingling quite independently of the Academy. We would rehearse outside school hours, and choose what plays we wanted to do; the Americans cast and directed them from first, second and third-year students. Bob Sloane decided to do *Hullo Out There* by William Saroyan. I was cast as the young girl and Brian Cox was the prisoner. Very briefly, the play deals with the relationship between the prisoner and the jailer's daughter. He's to be hanged, and she tries to rescue him by stealing a gun so that he can break out of gaol. I was thrilled to do it, found Brian good to work with, and was totally absorbed. We did one performance only, but it meant the world to me.

The next day I was back to the usual routine. We were rehearsing a Chekov play, and an actor started tapping the floor with a piece of wood. This was how we had started *Hullo Out There*, with the prisoner tapping the floor. Suddenly the play came flooding back to me and I thought, 'I've got to get the gun for him.' I ran out of the theatre, down the Earls Court Road to the main building, with one thought in my mind—to get the gun. I bumped into the director and stammered, 'The gun, I've got to get the gun!' Then I burst into tears—with a mixture of shock at my involvement and regret that something good had gone for ever.

This experience frightened me and I'm glad to say it's never happened again. Since then I have met actors who do live their parts twenty-four hours a day. I think this is very dangerous. The profession is so extraordinary and disorientating that one must work at real life, in much the same way as one must work at a good marriage.

Conversely, real life should continuously fuel one's acting. No experience, however awful or embarrassing, is useless to an actor. In one place I rented a room in the flat of a high-powered business woman. When Winston Churchill's funeral was on television she exhorted me to 'Come in, Anna dear, it's

educational. I'm sure you can spare a quarter of an hour.' She
always talked about Africa at breakfast. I've always been
dreadful at Geography, and dreaded these early morning
encounters. She was obsessively tidy, and this too was a threat.
Once, God knows why, I buttered and marmaladed my
Ryvita on her kitchen floor instead of her table. It might have
been a compliment to her spotless floor but I suspect that really
I was making an inner protest. Poor woman, she was perplexed
at her sticky floor, but though she mentioned it with increasing
irritation, I found it hard to break the habit. I managed to get
jam over the taps, too. I was aware that I was being awful and
wrote in my diary that I was becoming a 'dreadful person'.
When I played Abigail in *The Crucible*, I used her image as one
of the women I had to stick pins into, and at night rehearsed
spells in my room in which, without knowing it, she played a
starring role.

I did try to become a good citizen as well as actress. I enrolled
for Task Force and, with a fellow student, was given a list of
old people to visit. One old lady lived by Earls Court Station,
in a basement flat. The first time I visited her a large dog
answered the door. It was an enormous Alsatian. I saw a little
of the old lady behind him (like an unfinished jigsaw puzzle)
and asked if I could help her. She told me to come in, but this
was easier said than done. Not only was the dog huge, but very
suspicious of every bit of my anatomy. I managed somehow to
get down the passage by flattening myself against the wall and
sliding along it, with my hands protecting the parts of me that
aroused his greatest interest. Once in the sitting-room I was
appalled at the stench and filth. The old lady complained of the
heating bills and the mean landlord. Meanwhile the dog had
brought in a friend, a very small, scruffy mongrel and they
began to copulate on the carpet between us. I tried to concentrate on what she was saying. It was very hard. However, we
became very good friends—the old lady and I, I mean. The
dog and I were confirmed enemies. One day I arrived late.
She had asked me to get her some pills (anti-depressants I

think) and she was furious. 'Get out! Get out!' she cried. 'You don't care if I die—and don't come back at Christmas! I may not be here!' I felt dreadfully guilty because I had been late, and after a couple of sleepless nights, sent her an enormous bunch of flowers and all was well.

There were other occasions of a more exalted nature. I narrowly missed meeting the Queen. We students were invited to be usherettes at a charity performance of *Hullo Dolly* and everybody was very excited. We would be introduced to the Queen! I was overcome with pride when I was singled out to prepare the Red Carpet along which the royal feet would walk. So great was my excitement at this honour that having unrolled the shining, crimson pathway, I was promptly sick over it. A rather stout professional usherette fixed me with a beady glare. '*You* are *not* going to meet the Queen,' she said, and pushed me towards the exit so I wouldn't do any more damage to the royal carpet, while my fellow students got down to the unenviable task of removing any evidence that A.C.M. had been there.

One celebrity I did meet was Elizabeth Bergner. Our year was doing *The Cherry Orchard*. We each had to play two characters—thus I played Anya in the first and second acts, and Charlotta Ivanovna in the third and fourth. Celia Gore Booth played Anya in the third and fourth, and Charlotta at the beginning. We were both looking for a German accent to help us and Celia said casually one day, 'I know Elizabeth Bergner. We could go to tea today and just listen to her. Would you like to come?' I leapt at the opportunity. We were both wearing dirty jeans and looked pretty scruffy, but who cared! When we arrived at her front door a maid asked us in. She had a little white cap, like a cake decoration on her head, and a snow-white apron. She was just like a maid in a French farce. We were shown into the drawing-room. It was enormous, with very high walls, and magnificently furnished. Everything was white—white walls, white carpet, white book-cases, white tables, white sofas, white curtains. It was stunning. I felt very

out of place. Then Elizabeth Bergner came in, small, slender,
very beautiful, immaculately dressed in black, and in a husky
voice told us to make ourselves comfortable. We almost disappeared into the huge white sofa cushions.

She seemed to know why we had come; I thought she must
be psychic. Looking back, I'm sure that Celia's mother must
have told her why we wanted to see her, but then I preferred
the more dramatic explanation. Anyway, she was fascinating
and extremely frank. She talked about the theatre and Brecht
and plays she had been in. She handed us a beautiful box of
chocolates, very dark brown, and we each chose one. I've never
liked chocolates, but I thought maybe there was a waste-paper
basket I could drop it into. There wasn't. I looked desperately
around. By this time the chocolate had melted in my hot fist. I
could feel it running through my fingers. It was out of the
question to hide it somewhere in the sofa, so I just held it. It
was like a liquid magnet. Miss Bergner rose, indicating it was
time for us to leave. 'Please God, don't let her shake my hand!'
I backed nervously away, like some oriental maiden, thanking
her so very much for a marvellous time, and gratefully watched
the front door close as I wiped my filthy palm on my grubby
jeans.

In those days I was so absorbed in acting that love took a
back seat. I suppose normally at that age girls are taken up
with their burgeoning relationships with men. I had good
friends but no lovers. I was the only virgin in my year, and I
think it must have shown. One American fell in love with me
but was unfortunately allergic to me. He was a fat, dark,
curly-haired Jewish boy with 'hang ups' (his words) who
smoked a pipe. Whenever he felt amorous towards me he
couldn't stop sneezing. He broke ten pipes that way. I always
bought him new ones, as I felt it was my fault.

Another fellow student took me out one night to a beautiful
restaurant with wine and candles. I was a little puzzled, as he
had never shown any interest in me at classes. After we'd had a
glass of wine he began to ask me terribly personal questions,

which I refused to answer. Suddenly he confessed he was deeply in love with me. What was my reaction? he wanted to know. I laughed. 'Why are you telling me all this?' I asked. 'You don't care two hoots for me.' He then admitted that he was writing a play and had based the heroine on me—but he'd got stuck in the Second Act. He didn't know how I would react to a declaration of love, and that was why he was taking me out for this slap-up meal. I'm afraid he never finished the play.

I was also taken out by a very shy student. On our first date, after sitting in complete silence for ten minutes, he suddenly looked down at the table, and said, 'What are your chief interests?' I thought it sounded rather formal, but I answered him. Another silence fell. He looked down again. 'What do you care most about in life?' I told him, though again I was a bit surprised by his lack of spontaneity. 'Where do you go for your holidays?' he stuttered into his lap. 'What have you got down there?' I asked. 'What do you mean?' he said. 'There's something in your lap,' I said. He blushed and bought a tattered piece of paper from under the table. I took it from him. It was covered in questions to ask me. I felt so stupid. The idea that this man could be shy of me seemed ludicrous. Luckily we both laughed, and then chattered on into the night.

I had the usual student holiday jobs. For me they were especially important in enabling me to fill out my meagre experience of 'Life'. We had a teacher called Frieda Hodgson who exhorted us when working on a poem or part to 'live with it, eat with it, sleep with it!' One student took her literally and became pregnant and had to leave. I had Frieda's advice in mind when I took a vacation job as a barmaid at the Rugby Tavern in Twickenham. I was so busy going through parts in my head that I don't think I was really there. I poured pints with mountains of froth, like tiers on a wedding cake, and worked out the change more by imagination than by arithmetic. One evening a gentleman with a thick voice asked me for what sounded like a 'gin and booze'. This was a new one on me. I drew a gin and then asked the landlord where I could find 'the booze'. He looked at me very patiently and said, It's Booth's Gin, dear!' I had already strained his powers of endurance by causing several of the measures to malfunction. The final straw came when, in my efforts to become a more efficient barmaid, I slammed the till shut with such panache that it jammed with my cardigan in its teeth, imprisoning me and severely inhibiting business for two hours. I was given the sack.

It didn't really matter. A pub is one of the best places in the world to study characters. Most of them were middle-aged, but as I was often asked to play old ladies and inhibited spinsters, it was all fuel. This was what was so glorious about drama school. For three years I was able to play a wide variety of parts which I was often unsuited to, but I learnt a great deal. I look forward to playing the Nurse in *Romeo and Juliet* when I'm old, because I've already had a flavour of it. There is no other training I know of which prepares one for old age! No other chance to make a complete fool of oneself and not be judged accordingly. In fact the main thing they taught us was to dare to be bad. Oddly, when I left it was suddenly a shock to find I was an ingénue.

I had been very fortunate in being asked by Larry Dalzell in my first year to join his agency. He believed in starting one's career by a good hard stint in repertory theatre. It was then that LAMDA's training really started in earnest; I'd absorbed three years' teaching, and for the first few months I was adjusting to the reality of the theatre, the ephemeralness of it all, and putting into practice what I'd learnt by rote. LAMDA's insistence on always referring one's acting back to reality works like a yeast throughout one's career. One actor I know told me that *his* drama school taught 'Charm, charm, charm!' LAMDA's approach to text and characterization was founded on truth and not theatricality.

When I was playing Sonya in *Uncle Vanya* at the Royal Court, Tony Page told me that I should never give myself a moment to *think*: Sonya was always *doing*. So I concentrated on everything that I was doing physically—to prevent myself thinking. In one scene I had to pour tea for everybody. Unfortunately one night we had a leaking samovar which spilt all over the stage cloth. 'I must get something to mop it up,' I thought. I bent down and suddenly realized that the stage cloth represented grass: we were outside. Who would dream of wiping tea from the lawn? But this habit of referring back to reality I'd learnt from LAMDA.

Physically an actor never stops training. Groundwork at the Academy was excellent, but I was very clumsy. When I met Gregory de Polnay, a fellow student, again recently, he said, 'I thought you were always like a rugby player at LAMDA. I looked on you as a good scrum half.'

I was surprised but rather relieved. At LAMDA we had a class in which we were told to impersonate each other. This was to give us an objective idea of the public face we presented to the world—a disconcerting, if salutary experience. I'd always looked on myself as pretty earthy, with no silly frills. I was mortified when a student, imitating me, cast her eyes up to heaven and in a breathy voice simpered, 'Daisies, beautiful daisies.' This mimicry disturbed me, and I've never forgotten it. So it was good to know, albeit years later, that at least someone shared my own view of myself.

I tried desperately hard to be graceful, but even after three years' training I wasn't the world's best mover. One of my first professional experiences was playing Jennifer Dubedat in *The Doctor's Dilemma,* by Shaw. Peter Dews used to say, 'It's no good striding across the stage like Saint Joan leading her troops. You must glide, glide, *glide*—be a beautiful woman.' So one night I thought, 'I'll show him tonight I can do it!' I sailed across the stage with great style to sit at the head of the table, and completely missed the stool. One very thoughtful actor put his hand under my bottom so I wouldn't fall down. I sat on his out-stretched hand for five minutes, using it as a seat. It never occurred to me to exchange it for the stool I'd missed.

It's now ten years since I left drama school. Looking back

over those student days is very strange. It's like seeing someone else, who was totally absorbed in just one thing. There were no responsibilities outside of that. I was lucky to be able to do what I had dreamt about as a child. I had three God-given, happy, glorious, carefree years.